info@kinfolk.com
www.kinfolk.com

Kinfolk Magazine
328 NE Failing Street
Portland, Oregon 97212 USA
Telephone: 303-946-8400
Printed in Canada

Publication Design by Charlotte Heal
Cover Photograph by Pelle Crepin

KINFOLK

TOAST

WOMEN

MEN

HOUSE&HOME

NATHAN WILLIAMS
Editor in Chief & Brand Director

GEORGIA FRANCES KING	**CHARLOTTE HEAL**
Editor	*Creative Director*
GAIL O'HARA	**ANJA VERDUGO**
Managing Editor	*Art Director*
DOUG BISCHOFF	**KATIE SEARLE-WILLIAMS**
Business Operations	*Business Manager*
NATHAN TICKNOR	**JENNIFER JAMES WRIGHT**
Operations Manager	*Ouur Design Director*
JESSICA GRAY	**PAIGE BISCHOFF**
Community Director	*Accounts Payable & Receivable*
JESSE HIESTAND	**JOANNA HAN**
Web Administrator	*Contributing Editor*
AMANDA JANE JONES	**KELSEY SNELL**
Founding Designer	*Proofreader*
ANDREA SLONECKER	**ANNA LOH**
Recipe Editor	*Editorial Assistant*
SAMMI MASSEY	**MEGAN LAPLANTE**
Editorial Assistant	*Operations Assistant*
KATARINA BERGER	**SONYA TRACHSEL**
Operations Assistant	*Business Assistant*

———

SUBSCRIBE
KINFOLK IS PUBLISHED FOUR TIMES A YEAR
TO SUBSCRIBE, VISIT WWW.KINFOLK.COM/SUBSCRIBE OR EMAIL US AT SUBSCRIBE@KINFOLK.COM

CONTACT US
IF YOU HAVE QUESTIONS OR COMMENTS, PLEASE WRITE TO US AT INFO@KINFOLK.COM
FOR ADVERTISING INQUIRIES, GET IN TOUCH AT ADVERTISING@KINFOLK.COM

www.kinfolk.com

Frame: MYKITA NO1 SUN KUBICK | Photography: Mark Borthwick

MYKITA

HANDMADE IN BERLIN

MYKITA SHOPS Berlin, Cartagena, Monterrey, New York, Paris, Tokyo, Vienna, Zermatt, Zurich, **E-Shop** www.mykita.com

Ouur

ISSUE FIFTEEN CONTRIBUTORS

JONAS BJERRE-POULSEN
Photographer
Copenhagen, Denmark

RODRIGO CARDOSO
Photographer
Lisbon, Portugal

JAMES CARTWRIGHT
Writer
London, United Kingdom

LIZ CLAYTON
Writer
Brooklyn, New York

KATRIN COETZER
Illustrator
Cape Town, South Africa

PELLE CREPIN
Photographer
London, United Kingdom

ARADIA CROCKETT
Stylist
London, United Kingdom

TRAVIS ELBOROUGH
Writer
London, United Kingdom

MARGARET EVERTON
Writer
Portland, Oregon

MAIA FLORE
Photographer
Paris, France

ROSE FORDE
Stylist
London, United Kingdom

KATIE FOTIS
Stylist
London, United Kingdom

NICOLE FRANZEN
Photographer
Brooklyn, New York

ANDREW & CARISSA GALLO
Directors
Portland, Oregon

ALICE GAO
Photographer
New York, New York

GENTL & HYERS
Photographers
New York, New York

ALYX GORMAN
Writer
Sydney, Australia

ØYVIND HALSØY
Writer
Bergen, Norway

PANICHA IMSOMBOON
Writer
Hudson, New York

TARANEH JERVEN
Writer
Vancouver, BC, Canada

KRISTOFER JOHNSSON
Photographer
Stockholm, Sweden

STEPHANIE ROSENBAUM KLASSEN
Writer
Sonoma, California

BRIANNA KOVAN
Writer
Los Angeles, California

DAVID LAMB
Stylist
London, United Kingdom

SARAH MAYCOCK
Illustrator
Hastings, United Kingdom

TEC PETAJA
Photographer
Nashville, Tennessee

JULIE POINTER
Writer
Portland, Oregon

GLEN PROEBSTEL
Prop Stylist
New York, New York

SARAH ROWLAND
Writer
Nashville, Tennessee

KATHERINE SACKS
Writer
Berlin, Germany

MARK SANDERS
Photographer
London, United Kingdom

ANDERS SCHØNNEMANN
Photographer
Copenhagen, Denmark

NATHALIE SCHWER
Stylist
Copenhagen, Denmark

RYO SHIRAI
Photographer
Tokyo, Japan

PER OLAV SØLVBERG
Stylist
Bergen, Norway

JOHN STANLEY
Writer
London, United Kingdom

ANNU SUBRAMANIAN
Writer
New York, New York

AARON TILLEY
Photographer
London, United Kingdom

RAHEL WEISS
Photographer
London, United Kingdom

SASHA FEDULOW WIRTH
Writer
Sydney, Australia

PEGGY WONG
Photographer
San Francisco, California

DIANA YEN
Writer & Food Stylist
New York, New York

WELCOME

———

We're all budding entrepreneurs in one way or another, whether we own a small business, have grand plans for starting one or just enjoy daydreaming about throwing caution to the wind to make donuts full-time. No matter if you're working in an artistic field as a maker and doer, crunching numbers or saving lives, creativity can be found in all our pursuits. For the Entrepreneurs Issue of *Kinfolk*, we explore the motivation and innovation that drives the spirit of entrepreneurship in our workplaces, as well as provide inspiration to balance our regular workdays with more leisure time.

We've dedicated 20 pages to showcasing 25 business owners who are building and strengthening communities. From peer-to-peer bike sharing to crowd-sourced beer brands, these creators have a knack for serving their customers by helping them connect with both their neighbors and the greater community.

The remarkable author and philosopher Alain de Botton talks with us about the nature of career satisfaction, the founders of the online photography network VSCO and the portfolio website Behance explain how they interact with their digital communities offline, and Hans Ulrich Obrist, one of the world's most renowned curators, tells us how he arranges the items on his bedside table.

But only focusing on the time we spend at our desks wouldn't represent everything else that goes into creating a productive mind-set: Like a pie cooling on a window sill, to fixate on the results would discount the effort (and butter) that goes into the finished product. The decisions we make at home and at play can influence the mentality we enter our workdays with, so we offer an essay on Sunday night routines that will make your evening a cheerier hue than blue, a photo essay on the importance of escaping from your ordinary influences to see the world from a different angle and explorations into the scientific benefits of both doodling and list making.

And how could we forget that happy little helper that many entrepreneurs cannot do without? Coffee. Instead of limiting ourselves to just a mug, we've dedicated a whole menu to the ways we can eat it too—Chocolate-Covered Espresso Bean Brownies, anyone?

When we want to make a change in the world, we can sometimes feel pressured to keep achieving when what we really need is a break to slow down and focus on our personal goals. After all, it can be hard toeing the priority line between work and play. So we're thrilled to present an excerpt from Carl Honoré's book *In Praise of Slowness*, as well as a feature interview with the Slow monarch on how to decelerate our sped-up lives.

While *Kinfolk* often focuses on the choices we make outside of work hours, this issue gives the same mindful attention to the time spent improving our professional selves. As mom would say, "If you love what you do, you'll never have to work another day in your life."

———

NATHAN WILLIAMS AND GEORGIA FRANCES KING

Community

All jobs eventually come down to serving our communities in one way or another: Whether creating life-affirming products or valuable services, businesses help shape the way we see our neighborhoods.

Home

There's nothing more comforting than coming home to the scent of freshly cooked dinner and the sight of a comfy couch. In order to recharge for the days ahead, solid downtime in your abode is key.

Work

Whether you spend your days in front of a screen, a canvas or in a field, there are plenty of opportunities to find creativity and fulfillment in your professional life. Just don't take yourself too seriously.

Play

The time you spend outside of the office influences the quality of the hours you put in at your desk. These moments should be respites to reinvigorate your mind as well as soothe your body.

Food

One of the ways to periodically break up your workday is by snacking. Taking the time to share a meal with your coworkers away from your desks will prepare your stomach and mind for the rest of the day.

Starters

COMPILED BY
GAIL O'HARA

Defining the Entrepreneur

We asked a number of enviable business minds how they define the nature of entrepreneurship.

YOTAM OTTOLENGHI, CHEF, WRITER AND RESTAURATEUR:

Someone who has courage in their convictions, as well as the wisdom to listen when the details don't always go according to plan —and then changing them as a result. You need to hold the big picture's convictions at the same time as tweaking and tweaking the small details until they're right—it's having the energy of both the long-distance runner and the sprinter.

LAURA BALLANCE, COFOUNDER, MERGE RECORDS:

An entrepreneur is a creative person who endeavors to craft something that appeals to other people. You need to be creative, observant, brave and patient.

MICHAEL PREYSMAN, FOUNDER AND CEO, EVERLANE:

It means not being afraid to take risks and jump in headfirst. I meet people who feel the need to build skills before starting something on their own. That's a good philosophy, but at some point, it's time to let go and start the journey. I don't think there's just one way to be a good entrepreneur, but I've had three guiding principles: 1) Be willing to change. Building a business can be an incredible opportunity for self-improvement if you can be truly self-aware and open to feedback. 2) Always ask why. That means you can't shy away from challenging conventional wisdom in order to find the best answers. 3) Don't be afraid to fail. Things are always going to go wrong and once you accept this, it's easier to move forward.

MIKE THELIN, COFOUNDER, FEAST PORTLAND:

An entrepreneur is the ultimate creative person. It's not a synonym for a "businessperson," though the words are sometimes interchangeably. Authentic entrepreneurs create their own lives and their own rules and thrive on transforming ideas into things. People often mistakenly believe that entrepreneurs are driven by money, which is not usually true. An entrepreneur is driven by improvement, invention and always wanting to do something better. You can only measure success for yourself.

TAAVO SOMER, FOUNDER, FREEMANS SPORTING CLUB/FREEMANS:

It's an American spirit and that's what epitomizes us. We have a cowboy mentality to break off and set out on our own. Once you start, it's hard to stop trying new things. Not everybody has that discipline and not everybody is prepared to accept failure. If you want to start something, you have to have the endurance to do it for years: So many people have ideas for 30 seconds.

BLAKE MYCOSKIE, FOUNDER AND CHIEF SHOE GIVER, TOMS:

You must be creative, innovative and take smart risks. You must always be hungry for knowledge and ready to learn new things. It means you're ready to embrace the unknown. I've learned how to be creative with limited resources and use criticism to inspire my competitive edge. I've become more willing to face my fears and rise to challenges I've never faced before.

ILLUSTRATION: KATRIN COETZER

DUANE SORENSON, FOUNDER, STUMPTOWN COFFEE ROASTERS:

Somebody who gets their butt out of bed and tries to create something for their community or for their neighbors and is hopefully able to make a little dough out of it.

CHAD DICKERSON, CEO, ETSY:

Someone who takes risks to build and grow something. But the risk goes beyond the financial and is often deeply personal, emotional and artistic. Entrepreneurs are fearlessly committed to their craft, using their creative skills to make a life, not just a living. You have to have passion for what you're doing to get started, but passion alone isn't enough. It has to be supported by perseverance for the inevitable ups and downs of getting a business off the ground and running it, particularly a creative business where you have to match what you love doing with what the market wants. Finally, diligence is important. All of the successful entrepreneurs I've met in my career are incredibly hard workers with extraordinary commitment to their goals, even when things are incredibly difficult.

SETH GODIN, AUTHOR AND FOUNDER, SQUIDOO:

An entrepreneur builds something bigger than herself, combining insight with bounded risk and leadership with vulnerability. Their essential qualities are ego, lack of ego; risk-taking, fear of risk; certainty, vulnerability; knowledge, ignorance; and mostly, always moving, always learning, always creating... for someone else.

MORGWN RIMEL, DIRECTOR, THE SCHOOL OF LIFE:

It means someone who sees opportunity and the possibility for improvement where others might not and works to turn that potential into reality. They may be successful in their endeavor or they may fail, but the point is that they give changing the status quo a go. They share a particular mind-set—one typified by vision (the ability to see opportunities where others see problems), empathy (the ability to genuinely step into the shoes of others), flexibility/adaptability (knowing when to adapt and when to hold fast), discernment/rigor (being able to distinguish a good, actionable idea from a bad one), self-belief (a precarious tightrope between arrogance and under-confidence), a healthy approach to failure (the ability to take sensible risks and acknowledge mistakes, then learn from them and move forward) and determination/perseverance/grit (the ability to entertain the uncomfortable and keep going).

MAYA NUSSBAUM, EXECUTIVE DIRECTOR, GIRLS WRITE NOW:

Recognizing a need and coming up with a vision to meet it. Having a sustainable business, keeping quality high and meeting new needs requires adaptability and innovation.

VINCE LAVECCHIA, PARTNER/GENERAL MANAGER, INSTRUMENT:

Anyone who has an idea, believes he can do better and has the guts to start something. You also need to have truth, effort, courage and a good network of people who believe in you.

WORDS
STEPHANIE ROSENBAUM KLASSEN

The Science of Scribbling

Doodlers, rejoice! Scrawling stick figures and pyramids in afternoon meetings may actually make us concentrate more on the tasks at hand, not less.

John F. Kennedy drew sailboats. Ronald Reagan sketched cowboys, football players and hearts. Russian writer Fyodor Dostoyevsky filled his manuscript pages with images of buildings and faces. And Teddy Roosevelt, Dwight Eisenhower and Hillary Clinton: doodlers, all.

The urge to fight boredom with pattern and design is a near-universal habit. An otherwise somnolent brain kicks into gear when we're creating shapes and controlling symmetry. Our primal hunter-gatherer impulses, ever alert to the stealthy moves of predator and prey, weren't meant to function in complete vacuums. As any laptop-tapping coffee shop denizen can tell you, your focus sharpens when there's a low-level hum in the background keeping the neurons firing (hissing steam frothers, Devendra Banhart, the goofy ideas of those nearby app developers). Doodling, it seems, is the brain's way of creating its own café society.

We all doodle with subjects and styles that are unique and remarkably long lasting. What we drew on the covers of our middle school notebooks or scribbled in marker on our high school sneakers is probably strikingly similar to what we're sketching digitally on our tablets today. While it's tempting to wonder if all those spirals, alien heads or inky arrows could be pointing the way through the maze of our subconscious minds, a handful of scientific studies indicate that what we draw is less important than the act of drawing itself.

According to a study published in *Applied Cognitive Psychology* (and later reported by *The Lancet*, a leading British medical journal), subjects who were asked to memorize lists of names during a recorded telephone call while shading in shapes with a pencil had nearly 30 percent better memory retention than non-doodlers—a benefit that spilled over into similar subsequent tests. Jackie Andrade, the scientist who developed the study, theorized that doodling "stabilized [the brain's] arousal at an optimal level," boosting concentration by actually decreasing the brain's propensity to wander. This means that more doodling means less daydreaming (and given that more than half of all U.S. presidents have been habitual doodlers, that's probably a good thing).

Much like a bowl of M&Ms or the now-forbidden workplace cigarette, the sweet distraction of doodling can provide short-term respite from anxiety at the very least. Who hasn't channeled a case of nerves by scribbling snakes and ladders during a job interview phone call, or combined note taking with some tension-relieving caricatures of your bad-news boss?

In her 2011 TED Talk, doodling advocate Sunni Brown claimed that "doodling can have a profound impact on the way we can process information and the way we can solve problems," especially for predominantly visual learners. Sunni, author of *The Doodle Revolution*, says that businesses can flourish by promoting "info-doodling," a form of visual interpretation that combines words, pictures and patterns to create conceptual maps of strategies and ideas. There's also the satisfaction of creative expression when the stakes are low; even the clumsiest stick-figure artists among us should feel free to scrawl and sketch when a dreary conference call is droning on.

Considering all the benefits—relief of anxiety, the joy of creativity, renewed concentration and focus—why wait until you're on hold with the cable company or trapped in a sales meeting? Go ahead: Pick up a digital stylus, ballpoint or lead pencil and let your imagination roam.

WORDS
KATIE SEARLE-WILLIAMS

Learning to Unlearn

Sometimes opening our eyes to knowledge's blind spots can reveal fresh solutions to old problems and give us an appreciation for the unknown.

"You know, it's not the strongest or the smartest person but the one who's most flexible that survives, right?"
– *Often mistakenly attributed to Charles Darwin, paraphrased by my mom*

My mom isn't one to straight-up dish out advice to her children. Typically she lets us talk through our issues and then prompts us with questions that guide us to clarity, preferring to allow us to find solutions on our own. But there is one particular nugget of wisdom I can recall her openly admonishing on several occasions: "As I grow older, I'm continually gaining knowledge. It would make sense for that knowledge to accumulate or at least bolster up my IQ, but instead of exponentially becoming smarter, the more I learn, the more I realize how little I actually know."

She is pointing out a few things here: It isn't simply the breadth of your own knowledge that's essential, but rather an appreciation of the vastness of the unknown information that exists in the world. There are so many differing theories and philosophies circulating on any one topic. What once seemed black and white in our early years shifts to more of a gray area as we learn of alternative perspectives. Simultaneously, the speed of innovation presents the paradox of the 21ST century: Knowledge is important... until it is suddenly irrelevant and no longer is.

The practice of unlearning isn't about right or wrong—it's about being open and exploring what's underneath. It isn't necessarily bad to repeat the past, but when we're confronted with significant changes, succumbing to the security blanket of our old approaches can rob us of experiences and growth. Unlearning doesn't require you to discredit your experience or presume that your current knowledge will hinder success. Rather, it encourages you to remain open to different ways of getting things done.

There's a common assumption that the systems and procedures we use every day are in place for a reason, that checks and balances can't be streamlined further or have already been distilled into their simplest forms. But it's possible that what was once an effective process may no longer be the quickest or easiest method. When implementing changes, we're given the opportunity to approach a task creatively, think through the reasons things have been done a certain way and wonder how they can be improved. However, we tend to gravitate toward the comfortable and find it difficult to deal with information that conflicts with our current beliefs and tried-and-true methods. As a result, we may be spending valuable time in our personal and professional lives following erroneous procedures that are inefficient or holding us back.

My mother also says that everyone knows change is hard. It takes time to audit work flows, research and implement new skills, and it isn't easy to admit that there is room for growth. If we consider our habits as living organisms, then it's our responsibility to constantly tend to and grow them. When we unlearn, we should consider new questions and approach problems with deliberate naïveté by challenging paradigms, questioning assumptions and relearning what's most important to our careers and our lives.

Yoyuu

This Japanese word helps convey the idea of feeling ready for whatever the world might throw at you next.

TYPE: Abstract noun
LANGUAGE: Japanese
PRONUNCIATION: "yoh-yoo"
ETYMOLOGY: a combination of _yo_ (additional, extra) and _yuu_ (ample, abundance)
MEANING: _Yoyuu_ is the presence of a momentary pause that allows us to recharge and prepare for life's next event, whether it's a business meeting or brunch with a friend. It's an imagined space you take for yourself to arrange mental (or physical) clutter, allowing yourself to be poised and ready to accommodate the other necessities of the day. Yoyuu conveys the accompanying feeling of calmness when you're mentally prepared for challenge and change.
USE: In noun form, it represents a balancing act where external actions are guided by internal stability. A person or business may be described with admiration to have an air of yoyuu about them. As an adjective, yoyuu describes the clarity and confidence breathed into its subject's foundation, such as yoyuu time, yoyuu conversations or a yoyuu space.

The Psychology of List Making

Why do we feel the need to make a list for every occasion, from grocery items to plans for world domination?

Lists keep our daily affairs in order, but they can also be distilleries of our deeper intentions. Regardless of their contents, they say a lot more about us than simply what we need to get done: They portray our expectations, self-criticisms and anxieties. In pursuit of moral perfection, Benjamin Franklin once drafted a list of what he deemed the necessary virtues in life. But not all innovative people have been as lofty as Ben when it comes to list making: The Finnish architect Eero Saarinen's to-do list included changing the lightbulb; elsewhere he listed the characteristics of his wife that he found most favorable. Eccentric and banal lists alike testify to our desire to cultivate order out of the messy shards of the everyday, and there is much to be gained from transmuting our goals into brief notes on a piece of paper.

Psychologists have found that we're hard-wired to function better when we have a plan. In 1927, Russian psychologist Bluma Zeigarnik found that people recall unfinished tasks more accurately than finished ones. Psychologists R.F. Baumeister and E.J. Masicampo have since updated the so-called Zeigarnik effect when they discovered that people also perform better at one task once they've created a concrete plan for completing their other uncompleted tasks. Using this logic, it means you'll more keenly tackle writing your staff newsletter if you've already created a plan to categorize last week's emails afterward. By allotting yourself time to complete each task on your list, you'll engage more presently with what's at hand because you know the next activity will be given its own time in due course.

But sometimes even the most articulate and carefully crafted to-do lists can't save us from procrastination or from the temptation to whip up a batch of scones instead of paying our gas bill. On some days, you just want to accept defeat from your overwhelming list of unaccomplished chores, responsibilities and life goals.

Fortunately you can dispel anxiety over the unfinished entries of today's list by condensing your unfinished list for tomorrow. To-do lists often work best when they value quality over quantity—Henry David Thoreau advised us to keep our accounts on our thumbnail, the shorter the better. The visceral act of checking a box can provide an addictive sense of satisfaction, but the best to-do lists should only contain essential tasks rather than fodder that makes us feel accomplished and ultimately distracted from our goals.

For everything else, we can forgive ourselves for allowing the dynamism of life to take us off course. Besides, if accomplishing everything requires us to sacrifice a meaningful engagement with our activities, perhaps it would be better to drop what we're doing and make those scones after all.

WORDS
JOHN STANLEY

Colleague Camaraderie

It's not just the work you do inside the office that counts: Sometimes what goes on after hours makes all the difference to productivity and morale in the workplace.

Once upon a macho time, promotions were won and lost on golf courses and in squash-club locker rooms. In 1960s advertising land, all serious work had to be done in the morning because of the number of martinis that were consumed over lunch while entertaining clients—or merely gabbing with their colleagues.

Workplace socializing is a curious beast. Many studies have consistently shown that a social workplace is a productive workplace with happier, healthier and more motivated staff. While workday boozing in the West now usually happens after hours, you may have an evening session of bowling, poker or Frisbee in the park planned instead of taking up a whole corner of your local speakeasy with the sole intent of getting sloshed and gossiping about your boss.

In Japan, however, the deep attachment to your team means that socializing after work is more of an obligation than an option. And you may end up seeing your boss nude—weekend retreats to clothing-free hot spring baths are still part of some trades, and the phrase "naked relationships" means almost, but not quite, what you think it means. It seems like no serious business gets done in Japan until all parties have gotten blind drunk together: You know whether you can trust someone if you've seen them barely able to stand and belting out "Just Dance" in a karaoke booth at 3 a.m.

Employers have long been subjecting their staff to different forms of forcible jollification, and nothing strikes fear into employee hearts like the words "team-building exercise." But if risking your life on an assault course (or communal nudity) isn't your thing, you can still raise office spirits by taking the organization of your workplace's playdates into your own hands.

The office itself can be a social opportunity to foster a lightly competitive and proudly convivial atmosphere: If it's your turn to be the social secretary, you could encourage creative team play such as in-house gin crafting or company bake-offs. Try giving everyone a hardy green plant for their desk (perhaps a succulent that's able to stand up to the rigors of fluorescent lights and air-conditioning) and advise that it's their task to keep it alive and thriving—after all, plants soothe the eye and soul. Office book clubs are also increasingly popular, encouraging sparky debate instead of water-cooler chat.

But sports remain the gold standard in after-hours connectivity. They are quintessentially successful at cultivating trust: one of the greatest things on earth you can't buy. If you don't feel like taking up golf just yet, you could organize a ping-pong tournament or a sunny afternoon of croquet. By socializing with coworkers from other departments, floors or even other businesses, you can actually increase your own team's productivity. It's funny, but the time you spend not working might actually be the most important thing you do all day.

Kinfolk's take on Hans' bedside table: 90° Wall Lamp by Frama. Sandy Gray Bedspread Fabric by Tapet Café. Bed frame and step stool by IKEA, both painted in Farrow & Ball's color "Mole's Breath." Wall drawing by Auguste Rodin. Photograph by Christian Brunnström. Books by Wolfgang Tillmans, Nan Goldin, Egon Schiele, Daniel Graham and Francesco Clemente.

PHOTOGRAPH: ANDERS SCHØNNEMANN; STYLING: NATHALIE SCHWER

My Bedside Table: The Curator

Hans Ulrich Obrist, renowned critic, art historian and curator at the Serpentine Galleries in London, tells us how he assembles the objects next to his bed and shares a few of his early bird rituals.

I like morning rituals: They're a way of liberating time when you're not online yet. The artist Paul Chan calls it "delinking," which is super-important in an ever-connected world. Every morning when I wake up I read the late French Martinican writer Édouard Glissant for 15 minutes. He is a great inspiration. The morning hours and the moments before sleeping are the best moments to read.

I don't sleep very much. I once tried the da Vinci sleep schedule (also known as the polyphasic method), which means sleeping for 15 minutes every 3 to 4 hours 7 to 8 times a day, but it didn't prove to be sustainable or productive. Now I always go to bed at midnight and get up really, really, really early, around 5 a.m.

When I moved to London in 2006, I introduced one more morning ritual with urbanist Markus Miessen: It's called the Brutally Early Club. It can be difficult to find time to gather with friends—artists, architects, scientists—so we'd meet in a café at 6:30 a.m. to talk. Nobody can say they have a prior engagement at that time! It's a way to get everybody together when the city is completely empty.

Another one of my rituals is going to a bookstore and buying a book every day, so there are always books everywhere: on the bedside table, in the kitchen, piled in the office, even at my parents' house. There are at least 15 of them in my bedroom at one time.

I spend quite a lot of time in hotels. I was a freelance curator in the '90s and traveled the world living a nomadic existence. The curation of a bedroom is still very important, even when traveling. When you're basically never home, you start thinking about bedside tables differently. I always have magazines and books piled on them, and I love hotel stationery: It gets put in a suitcase, goes to the next city, then to the next city, and then ends up at home. I sometimes even go to a hotel to work in my own city because I can get distracted if I'm surrounded by too many things. Hotels give me new constraints.

Wherever I am, I always seem to have Post-it notes nearby. Curating is about junction-making and bringing things, people and objects together. So I put ideas on Post-its and put them all over the place—windows, furniture, wherever—so that they somehow enter new junctions. They help me sort out my own thoughts. I've started writing a diary, and I record myself for 10 or 15 minutes on a voice recorder too, so I always have one of them near me. I often lose pens and pencils, so the ones I have are always changing.

Apart from that, I have very little by my bed. I used to have an alarm clock, but now I use my phone for that. I don't have a specific reading light, but I do have one of Olafur Eliasson's Little Suns, which are small solar lamps that he helped design.

I've always thought I have a good work-life balance because I've always done the work I've wanted to do. But it's not all about work. There's a lot of liberated time in the day: a time for reading, writing, conversation and for being with friends.

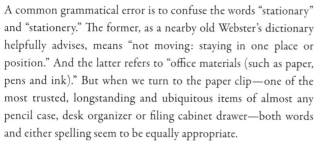

WORDS
TRAVIS ELBOROUGH

The Paper Clip: Original Simplicity

Sometimes perfection doesn't need improvement. Invented more than a century ago, the paper clip is a bastion for simplicity in design.

A common grammatical error is to confuse the words "stationary" and "stationery." The former, as a nearby old Webster's dictionary helpfully advises, means "not moving: staying in one place or position." And the latter refers to "office materials (such as paper, pens and ink)." But when we turn to the paper clip—one of the most trusted, longstanding and ubiquitous items of almost any pencil case, desk organizer or filing cabinet drawer—both words and either spelling seem to be equally appropriate.

In a world where even the crust of a humble takeout pizza can scarcely be left free from elaborate additions, the paper clip stands steadfast. Immune to fleeting fads, fashions and the mania for more and more innovative technology, its design has remained largely unchanged for close to a century now.

A perfectly turned loop-de-loop of steel wire that the French call a "trombone" in tribute to its curved form, the paper clip serves as potent and enduring emblem of the maxim "Less is more." It is perhaps the ultimate model of functional simplicity. It practically taunts us with its limber bendable body, unencumbered by pesky add-ons and free of updates or apps.

The paper clip first appeared in the late 19ᵀᴴ century, an era of expanding office bureaucracy and breakthroughs in the industrial production of steel. Although its precise origins are much disputed—there are rival claims for its invention hailing from Norway, America and England—sales brochures of the Victorian-era teem with a surprising array of different clip and pin products.

The style of paper clip that ultimately triumphed though is aptly called a Gem. Cheaper to manufacture and simpler to use than other often fiddlier models, the Gem proved to be a proficient and extremely cost-efficient clip to mass-produce. One early sighting of the Gem-style paper clip is in a patent filed by William Middlebrook of Connecticut in 1899 for a pin and clip making "machine." According to Henry Petroski's *The Evolution of Useful Things*, the name comes from a British company credited with making paper clips as early as the 1880s, though the style of the clip itself predates that. By 1908, the firm was able to proclaim the Gem as "the most popular clip" in America.

Despite the arrival of countless alternatives for fasteners, plastic coatings, colors and squarer-headed loops—not to mention hot desk-ing and paperless offices—the Gem's popularity has hardly wavered since. In fact, in complicated times, we can take solace in the paper clip's design, which handily enough can be bent or unraveled to double as something of a worry bead in moments of stress.

Pop a paper clip in your purse or pocket if you ever need to be reminded that the simpler stuff is usually the best. When you get something this right the first time around, standing still can be its own innovation.

WORDS
ANNU SUBRAMANIAN

Creative Constraints

Embracing our limitations and narrowing our focus is often exactly what's needed to free our minds.

"The possibilities are endless." It's a mantra we repeat to reassure, inspire, empower. It makes us feel like the world is an all-you-can-eat buffet and offers us the thrill we felt as kids of spinning a globe and promising to visit whatever fabled land our fingers landed upon.

But sometimes "endless possibilities" means an empty Word document with the cursor blinking like an impatiently tapping foot. It means a group brainstorm with open-ended questions that render participants silent and fretful. It means anxiety induced from too much variety in the breakfast cereal aisle or too many tabs open in your internet browser.

Suddenly, we find ourselves overwhelmed by the endlessness of endlessness. When faced with too many options we can freeze up or simply not act at all. We become paralyzed by the variety before us and the fear that we might choose the wrong option, whether it's a flavor of yogurt or your company's new name. While we sometimes benefit from having infinite choices, there are also benefits to limiting possibilities, even briefly.

The Oulipo Compendium is a testament to creative boundaries. In search of untapped creativity, these mid-20TH-century French artists forced bizarre restrictions upon themselves, developing radically new perspectives on old styles: Oulipo writer Georges Perec even once challenged himself to write *La Disparition*—a 300-page novel about the letter "E"—without ever using the vowel.

Of course we're not always looking to invent genre-bending works of art: Sometimes it's just an impending deadline or a weekend to-do list that leaves us feeling helpless. When we decrease our scope, our knowledge and awareness of what's before us grows.

Asking yourself "How can I be a better person?", "How do I start the great American novel?" or "What will be the next record-breaking internet start-up?" is like talking into the ether. Instead of trying to change your life in a day, start by isolating a part you can improve on, such as keeping the stove top clean or remembering to water the herbs. Instead of having the pressure of 300,000 unwritten words of literary genius looming above you, discover more about your lead character's personality by considering the way they would make a sandwich. Instead of being frustrated that you haven't invented the next Instagram, consider small ways you could digitally improve on a facet of your life.

Entrepreneurship isn't always a flash of genius from a dark corner of the mind: We gradually shed more and more light until the solution is dazzlingly clear. Constraints can inspire clarity, and then creativity. One of the best feelings when creating something new is how infinite we feel while doing it. But in order to reach that point, we sometimes have to be just the opposite.

The possibilities are endless, they really are. Unless, of course, you don't want them to be.

WORDS
GEORGIA FRANCES KING

Fusion Businesses

*Why is it that we always seem to crave
a stiff drink while doing the laundry?
Some cunning stores are combining two
business ideas into one with great success.*

We live in an era when we're expected to diversify rather than do one thing and do it well. Gone are the days of being able to luxuriate in focusing our efforts on a single skill, instead replaced by the assumption that in a diversified world, everyone should wear multiple hats (and update your company's social media feeds, too).

This has led to a smattering of all types of double dippers, such as the designer / directors, singer / songwriters, the actor / waiters and the masseuse / comedian / musician / dog-walker / mortgage brokers. Sometimes affectionately known as "slashies" due to their use of non-committal punctuation marks to define their careers, these people have recently extended their professional ambivalence to the public sector in the form of brick-and-mortar shop fronts.

Have you ever felt like a beer midway through a long day of shopping or become ravenous while sitting in the hairdresser's chair? Fusion businesses take two unrelated products or services and merge them together into one venture. Through taking a normally humdrum task and adding a gimmick, shop owners allow customers to tick off multiple to-do items in one fell swoop—and have a jovial time while doing so.

One of the most popular examples is the rise of the laundromat-bar. Instead of sitting and watching your socks tumble in circles, some smart hygienists decided to give consumers something else to do during their load—such as drinking! They have some great pun-ish names too, such as Brainwash in San Francisco and the Bar of Soap in Asheville, North Carolina. Not only do their beverage profits stay under one roof instead going to the pub down the road, but it also encourages you to interact with your neighbors instead of putting your nose into a tattered two-year-old copy of *Reader's Digest*.

Other normally tedious tasks can be made much more exciting when plied with alcohol. The Dressing Room in New York allows you to sip an Old Fashioned while looking through vintage threads, a string of cocktail lounges called Beauty Bar offers a martini and manicure deal, and Sycamore in Brooklyn will provide you with a beer and a bouquet for ten bucks.

But if drinking isn't your thing, some store owners provide purchase-fueling caffeine for their customers instead. Maker's Café in London offers 3-D printing services along with beverages, Golden Sound in Nashville offers a great selection of records, and there are numerous bike and motorcycle shops such as See See in Portland, Oregon, and Look Mum No Hands! in London that serve lattes.

Another activity that leaves you with some spare time to fill is being at the hairdresser: You can grab a bowl of bibimbap while your bangs are trimmed at a Korean café called Hurwundeki in London, a shot of whiskey with your whiskers at the Modern Man Barber Shop in Portland, Oregon, a tattoo with your trim at Graceland in Brooklyn or a shirt with your snip at Freemans Sporting Club in New York and Tokyo.

For other business owners, it's all about utilizing space. At Fuglen in Oslo, Norway, Thai Teak in Los Angeles and Red Door Yum Cha in Melbourne, Australia, you can have a tasty meal—and then purchase the furniture you ate it on. Others provide two commonly paired items under one roof, such as Baltimore's Ma Petite Shoe, where you can indulge in the bereaved post-breakup urge to purchase both chocolate and shoes simultaneously.

If you'd consider yourself a slashie and want to start a fusion enterprise, there are plenty of untapped markets waiting to be taken over, such as a liquor store/psychiatrist office, combination human/dog salons and an artist studio/unemployment agency. Or, for the more health-conscious, maybe you could open up a bicycle studio in the back of your laundry instead of a bar—and call it Spin Cycle. You're welcome.

PHOTOGRAPH: AARON TILLEY; STYLING: KATIE FOTIS

The Lunch Box:
Simple Tortilla
Española

———

Also known as a Spanish Omelet, this tasty dish can be prepared the night before and will provide all the carbohydrates and protein you need to make it through the rest of your workday. Serving suggestion: Eat away from your desk!

1 tablespoon extra-virgin olive oil

1 small Yukon Gold potato (about ¼ pound/115 grams), peeled, quartered and cut into ⅛-inch (3-millimeter) slices*

½ medium yellow onion, halved and thinly sliced

Salt and freshly ground pepper

1 tablespoon unsalted butter

4 large eggs

Pinch of nutmeg

In a 10-inch (25-centimeter) nonstick skillet, heat the oil over medium heat. Add the potato and onion and season generously with salt and pepper. Cook, stirring occasionally, until the potatoes and onions are translucent and very tender, 8 to 10 minutes. Transfer the potatoes and onions to a bowl and wipe the skillet clean.

In the same skillet, melt the butter over medium-low heat. Beat the eggs with the nutmeg and pour them into the pan. Cook undisturbed for 1 minute, then spread the potato and onion mixture over half of the eggs in an even layer. Continue cooking until the edges are set and the top is almost set but still moist, 5 to 7 minutes.

Using a spatula, fold the omelet in half to cover the filling, and then fold in half again. Remove the torta from the skillet and let it cool, then cut it in half and pack for lunch.

A traditional Tortilla Española contains potatoes and onions, but feel free to experiment with other vegetables such as slivered bell peppers or sliced button mushrooms.

32

PHOTOGRAPH: MAIA FLORE

WORDS
GAIL O'HARA

Work on Your Shoulders

Some people complain of life sitting on their shoulders, but for others it's work that provides that pressure.

When you start to feel the crushing weight of work stress on your tender shoulders, it's time to figure out a plan for knocking it off. We're all guilty of carrying our work home—even after a long day of slumping in an ergonomically incorrect seat as fluorescent lights sear our eyes and we carpal tunnel our way to wrist cramps—but how can we avoid doing it? First of all, looking after yourself is all up to you—it's important to take your health and well-being into your own hands, to selfishly take time to *not* think of work, to store your phone out of reach and to protect yourself from the barrage that work will push on you if you let it. According to Brian Luke Seaward, the author of *Managing Stress: Principles and Strategies for Health and Well-Being*, many ways to fight stress involve deep breathing and heartbeat variation exercises such as yoga, meditation, sleep, laughter and walking. Another way to get your mind off the screen, clear your head and open your eyes is to gaze upon nature. Seeing pretty things—trees, gardens, water and the sky—will help stressful feelings fall away. You may not be able to control everything that happens to you in life, but you can control your reaction to it. So when something happens, breathe. And if you still feel the crushing weight on your shoulders, do a shoulder stand.

WORDS
SASHA FEDULOW WIRTH

A Sense of Wander

When met with creative block, sometimes all you have to do is lace up your shoes and take to the sidewalk.

On a walk around London, Jane Austen came upon a portrait that brought her beloved character Jane Bennet to life in *Pride and Prejudice*. A stroll along the countryside of Vienna gave Ludwig van Beethoven the rustic melody of his *Pastoral Symphony*. Meandering through a Budapest park, Nikola Tesla had a flash of insight on how to tweak alternating currents to build an AC generator. Only by stepping away to stretch their legs did these creative entrepreneurs come across the inspiration that helped shape their greatest works.

The length of time away from their workspace varied, as did their pace and whether they greeted the morning sun or slipped out after supper. It was the activity itself—putting one foot in front of the other —that provided distance from the tangles of a problem and brought them closer to a clarity unavailable bound to a chair.

In a world of deadlines and endless meetings, penciling in time for an afternoon sojourn can seem indulgent, even wasteful. Yet stagnation in all its varied forms—staring blankly at a screen, rehashing the same ideas, settling for a mediocre solution—is a far more insidious thief. It not only steals minutes, but also pilfers productivity and efficiency in the process.

A destination for your stroll is optional. Albert Einstein favored his local beach. Steve Jobs did laps around the corporate park. Some days might call for staying close, others for venturing further and taking in new sights: After all, if Charles Dickens hadn't traded his usual London route for the marshlands of Kent, the vivid opening of *Great Expectations* may never have been penned.

Whether it's along paved roads or through overgrown brush, on city streets or around harbor promenades, casual meandering stimulates the senses and frees the mind to roam. The unusual hue of wildflowers becomes the color palette for a new website. Gauzy clouds and grainy sandstone inspire the texture of a photo shoot. The manic laughter of a magpie turns into the signature snicker of a novel's villain. But even if bolts of inspiration don't strike or solutions don't surface, the walk isn't in vain: The chance to set aside worries, shake off fatigue and buoy a faltering mood is reason enough to wander.

As the body loosens and reengages with the outside world, the chatter of the mind relaxes and settles. Distracted thinking is replaced with intuitive contemplation. Soon reactive thoughts fall gently by the wayside and deeper ones appear as signposts nudging us in the right direction. It is then that we return to our workspaces with inspired words to write, energized melodies to compose and new designs to sketch—all discovered along the way, step by step.

WORDS
MARGARET EVERTON

The Solace of Sunday Night

Whether you're planning the week's agenda or loafing on the couch, this evening can be used to embrace the calm before the weekdays' storm.

When formed with purpose, Sunday night can become a sanctuary. The practice of preparing for the week ahead can improve the quality of the weekday work itself. The poet Henry Wadsworth Longfellow once described these evenings as "the golden clasp that binds together the volume of the week." But what should be an evening of anticipated freedom and rejuvenation often leaves many bummed out about life's recurring responsibilities.

The "Sunday night blues" may sound like a quaint colloquialism, but it's actually the nickname for a real condition brought on by anxiety concerning the forthcoming weekdays. A study by the University of Gothenburg in Sweden determined that Sunday evening is the unhappiest time of the week, with Monday morning coming in a close second. You may treat this time like any other, but isolating a few hours to focus on the week ahead can paint a potentially bluish evening a livelier color.

Two kinds of combatants successfully resist the Sunday Night Blues: the toiler and the idler. The toiler jump-starts her upcoming schedule by accomplishing tasks on Sunday evening that may get jumbled during the week. Such proactivity can take countless forms: a college student congregates with roommates to prepare reheatable dinners for rushed days; a yogi lays out a row of clothes for each morning practice; and a business consultant conducts solitary planning meetings to organize his days. Each toiler transforms daily minutiae into a graceful pattern of living in his or her own way.

Meanwhile, the idler preserves this time for recharging the spirit. As *Treasure Island* author Robert Louis Stevenson championed in his essay "An Apology for Idlers," these types avoid extreme busyness by doing what modern society might consider to be wasting time. Eliminating "to-dos" creates guiltless space for unquantifiable experiences such as evaluating the larger portrait of life or spending time in the company of family and friends (or in rarified solitude). The idler naps or loafs around and invites an inner stillness by moving with no set pace or purpose: a psychologist dines with friends, a lawyer turns off her screen and reads for pleasure and a translator in Paris strolls through the Left Bank.

Regardless of whether you're a toiler or an idler, what you choose *not* to do with these hours can be just as important as what you choose to do: Omission is as important as permission. This interlude should have no agenda, no expectations and no one to answer to—and that includes feeling guilt-free when you veer from your usual routine. Sometimes you work all night or blow these hours on some mindless television show, but even the motion toward a conscious Sunday evening can improve the week ahead and enrich the overall tone of life. These hours can be a little blue, but they also can be blissfully rosy.

Entrepreneurs

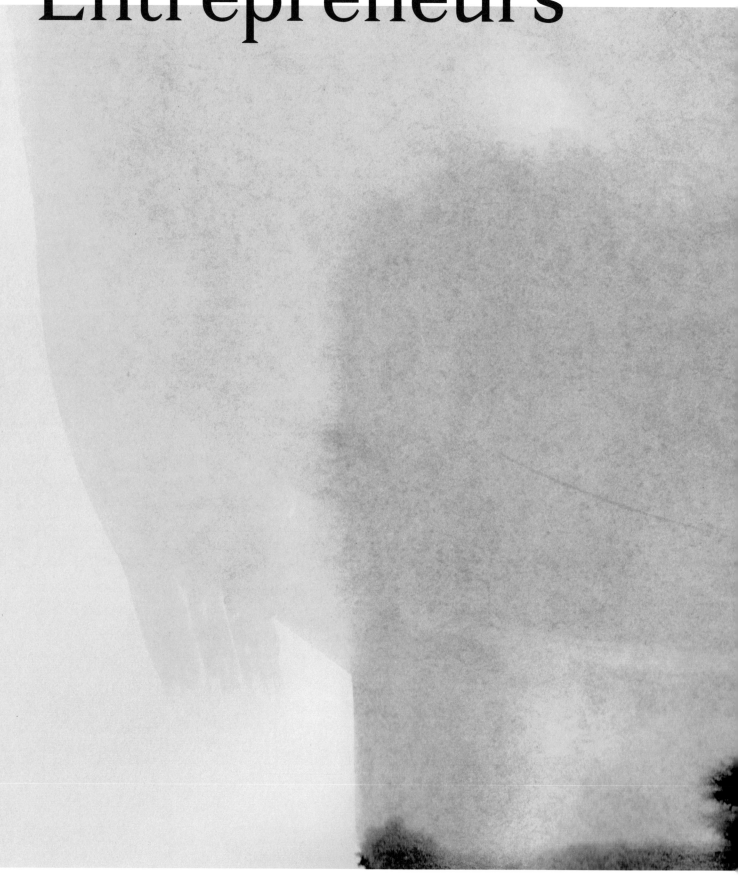

WORDS
CARL HONORÉ

PHOTOGRAPHS
MARK SANDERS

STYLING
DAVID LAMB

IN PRAISE OF SLOWNESS

When buzzing through a sped-up world where there are always battles to be won and emails to be answered, learning to slow down in the workplace is imperative to both our productivity and happiness. In this excerpt from Carl Honoré's book In Praise of Slowness: Challenging the Cult of Speed, he writes about the benefits of flexible hours and the importance of downtime.

There was a time, not so long ago, when mankind looked forward to a new Age of Leisure. Machines promised to liberate everyone from the drudgery of work. Sure, we might have put in the odd shift at the office or factory, monitoring screens, twiddling dials, signing invoices, but the rest of the day would be spent hanging out and having fun. With so much free time on our hands, words like "hurry" and "haste" would eventually fall out of the language.

Benjamin Franklin was among the first to envision a world devoted to rest and relaxation. Inspired by the technological breakthroughs of the latter 1700s, he predicted that man would soon work no more than four hours a week. The 19TH century made that prophecy look foolishly naive. In the dark satanic mills of the Industrial Revolution, men, women and even children toiled for 15 hours a day. Yet at the end of the 19TH century, the Age of Leisure popped up once again on the cultural radar. George Bernard Shaw predicted that we would work two hours a day by 2000.

The dream of limitless leisure persisted through the 20TH century. Dazzled by the magical promise of technology, the man in the street dreamed of a life spent lounging by the pool, waited on by robots that not only mixed a mean martini but also kept the economy ticking over nicely. In 1956, Richard Nixon told Americans to prepare for a four-day workweek in the "not too distant future."

A decade later, a US Senate subcommittee heard that by 2000 Americans would be working as little as 14 hours per week. Even in the 1980s, some predicted that robotics and computers would give us all more free time than we would know what to do with.

Could they have been more wrong? If we can be sure about anything in the 21ST century, it is that reports of the death of work have been greatly exaggerated. Today, the Age of Leisure looks as feasible as the paperless office. Most of us are more likely to put in a 14-hour day than a 14-hour week. Work devours the bulk of our waking hours. Everything else in life—family and friends, sex and sleep, hobbies and holidays—is forced to bend around the almighty work schedule.

In the industrialized world, the average number of hours worked began a steady decline in the middle of the 1800s, when six-day weeks were the norm. But over the past 20 years, two rival trends have taken hold.

While Americans work as much as they did in 1980, Europeans work less. By some estimates, the average American now puts in 350 hours more on the job per year than his European counterpart. In 1997, the US supplanted Japan as the industrialized cou with the longest working hours. By comparison, Europe lo a slacker's paradise. Yet even there the picture is mixed.

By some estimates, the average American now puts in 350 hours more on the job per year than his European counterpart.

with the fast-paced, round-the-clock global economy, many Europeans have learned to work more like Americans.

Behind the statistical averages, the grim truth is that the millions of people are actually working longer and harder than they want to, especially in Anglo-Saxon countries. One in four Canadians now racks up more than 50 hours a week on the job, compared to one in ten in 1991. By 2002, one in five thirtysomething Britons was working at least 60 hours a week. And that's before one adds in the long hours we spend commuting.

Whatever happened to the Age of Leisure? Why are so many of us still working so hard?

Beyond the great productivity debate lies what may be the most important question at all: What is life for? Most people would agree that work is good for us. It can be fun, even ennobling. Many of us enjoy our jobs—the intellectual challenge, the physical exertion, the socializing, the status. But to let work take over our lives is folly. There are too many important things that need time, such as friends, family, hobbies and rest.

For the Slow movement, the workplace is a key battlefront. When the job gobbles up so many hours, the time left over for everything else gets squeezed. Even the simple things—taking the kids to school, eating supper, chatting to friends—become a race against the clock. A surefire way to slow down is to work less. And that is exactly what millions of people around the world are seeking to do.

Everywhere, and especially in the long-hours economies, polls show a yearning to spend less time on the job. In a recent international survey by economists at Warwick University and Dartmouth College, 70 percent of people in 27 countries said they wanted a better work-life balance. In the US, the backlash against workaholism is gathering steam. More and more blue-chip firms, from Starbucks to Walmart, face lawsuits from staff allegedly forced to put in unpaid overtime. Americans are snapping up books that show how a more

leisurely approach to work, and to life in general, can bring happiness and success. Recent titles include *The Lazy Way to Success*, *The Lazy Person's Guide to Success* and *The Importance of Being Lazy*. In 2003, US campaigners for shorter working hours held the first national Take Back Your Time Day on October 24, the date when, according to some estimates, Americans have worked as much as Europeans do in a year.

Continental Europe has moved furthest down the road to cutting work hours. The average German, for instance, now spends 15 percent less time on the job than in 1980. Many economists reject the claim that working less creates more jobs by spreading the work around. But everyone agrees that trimming work hours generates more time for leisure, traditionally a higher priority among continental Europeans. In 1993, the EU laid down a maximum workweek of 48 hours with workers given the right to work longer if they wish. At the end of the decade, France took the boldest step so far to put work in its place by cutting the workweek to 35 hours.

In practice, France stipulated that no one should work more than 1,600 hours per year. Since the implementation of *les 35 heures* was negotiated at the company level, the impact of workers varies. Many French people now work shorter days throughout the year, while others work the same or even longer weekly hours but get extra days off. A mid-ranking French executive can aspire to nine weeks or more of annual vacation. Though some professions—among them senior business executives, doctors, journalists and soldiers—are exempted from the 35-hour rule, the net effect is a leisure revolution.

For many French people, the weekend now starts on Thursday, or ends on Tuesday. Legions of office staff desert their desks at 3 p.m. While some use the extra leisure time to veg out—sleeping or watching TV—many more have broadened their horizons. Enrollment in art, music and language classes has risen sharply. Tour operators report a boom in short trips to London, Barcelona and other European hot spots.

Everything else in life—family and friends, sex and sleep, hobbies and holidays—is forced to bend around the almighty work schedule.

Bars and bistros, cinemas and sports clubs are packed with people. The surge in leisure spending gave the economy a much-needed shot in the arm. But beyond the economic numbers, the shorter workweek has revolutionized people's lives. Parents spend longer playing hours with their children, friends see each other more often, couples have more time for romance. Even that favorite French pastime, adultery, has benefited. Paul, a married accountant in southern France, tells me that the 35-hour workweek allows him to indulge in an extra tryst each month with his mistress. "If cutting the workload gives more time for love, then it has to be a good thing, *n'est-ce pas?*" he says, with a wolfish grin.

Fans of the new regime are certainly easy to find. Take Emilie Guimard. The Paris-based economist now enjoys a couple of three-day weekends a month, on top of her six weeks of annual paid vacation. She has taken up tennis, and started reading the Sunday edition of *Le Monde* from cover to cover. Many of her long weekends are spent touring museums across Europe. "I now have time for things that make my life richer, and that is good for me and for my employers," she says. "When you are relaxed and happy in your personal life, you work better. Most of us in the office feel we are more efficient on the job than we used to be."

Many bigger companies have grown to love the 35-hour week. On top of the tax breaks they received for hiring more workers, the new regime allowed them to negotiate more flexible ways of working. Staff at large manufacturers, such as Renault and Peugeot, have agreed to work longer hours when production peaks and shorter hours when it slumps.

So the Cassandras who warned that the 35-hour week would send the French economy into instant meltdown have been proved wrong. The gross domestic product has grown, and unemployment, though still above the EU average, has fallen. Productivity also remains high. Indeed, some evidence suggests that many French workers are more productive now. With

less time on the job and more leisure to look forward to, they make greater efforts to finish their work before clocking off.

Yet working less is just part of the Slow blueprint. People also want to decide *when* they work. They want control over their own time—and businesses who grant it to them are reaping the benefits. In our time-is-money culture, giving workers dominion over the clock goes against the grain. Ever since the Industrial Revolution, the norm has been to pay people for the hours they spend on the job rather than for what they produce. But rigid timetables are out of step with the information economy, where the boundary between work and play is much more blurred than it was in the 19TH century. Many modern jobs depend on the kind of creative thinking that seldom occurs at a desk and cannot be squeezed into fixed schedules. Letting people choose their own hours, or judging them on what they achieve rather than on how long they spend achieving it, can deliver the flexibility that many of us crave.

Studies show that people who feel in control of their time are more relaxed, creative and productive. In 2000, a British energy company hired management consultants to streamline the shift system at its call center. Almost overnight, productivity nose-dived, customer complaints shot up and staff began leaving. By denying employees a say in when they worked, the new regime had ruined morale. Realizing its mistake, the company promptly gave the staff more control over its shifts, and soon the call center was more productive than ever. Many of the workers said that having "time autonomy" at work helped them feel less hurried and stressed both on and away from the job. Karen Domaratzki bears witness to that at Royal Bank of Canada: "When you have control over your own time, you feel more calm in everything you do."

I know this to be true from my own experience. In 1998, after years of freelancing, I joined the staff of a Canadian newspaper as the London correspondent. In an instant, I lost control of my time. Because I had no set working hours, I was, in theory, available 24/7. Even when my editors didn't call, there was always the chance that they might. The difference in time zones meant that assignments often landed on my desk in the afternoon, leaving me just a few hours before it was time to help put my son to bed. This meant a mad dash to finish, or reading Dr. Seuss with work hanging over me. It was miserable. At the time, I found other reasons to explain why a job I had loved so much had become such a millstone. My editor was small-minded. The paper covered stories in the wrong way. The hours were too long. When I began investigating the Slow movement, however, it became clear to me that the underlying problem was that I had lost the power to decide *when* to work. So why did I stick with it for nearly three years? My reasons were the same as those that prevent many of us from leaving jobs that make us unhappy: the fear of losing a good salary, of damaging my career, of disappointing others. Eventually, the decision to leave was made for me. When the paper announced mass layoffs, I was on the list—and over the moon.

Things are so much better now. I still work the same number of hours, sometimes even more, but my relationship with time is healthier. Now that I control my own schedule, I move through the working day feeling less hurried and resentful. And away from my desk, whether reading bedtime stories or preparing the evening meal, I am less liable to seek a shortcut. Sure, my earnings are down, but that's a small price to pay for enjoying my work—and my life—again. My only regret is that I didn't go back to freelancing sooner.

Of course, giving people control over their own time in the workplace will require a seismic shift in thinking. But where practical, it can—and should—be done. If deployed in the right spirit, information technology can help us do it. Instead of using Blackberrys, laptops and cell phones to extend the workday, we can use them to rearrange it. Many companies are already ceding more time autonomy to their staff. In the UK, for example, British Telecom, Bayer and Lloyds TSB now allow employees to customize their own schedules: to work from home, say, or to come in and leave the office at more convenient hours. Though it naturally lends itself more to white-collar work, time autonomy is also making inroads in the blue-collar world. Some Swiss watch factories have rearranged production to allow workers on a single shift to vary their start and finish times by up to three hours. In Gloucestershire, a nylon factory lets the staff set its own hours as long as at least two workers are on duty at all times.

The benefits of working less, and working when it's convenient, are clear enough, but now let's consider why it sometimes makes sense to work more slowly. In the just-in-time, modern workplace, speed seems to be all-important. Email and cell phones demand an instant response, and a deadline lurks around every corner. A 2001 survey conducted by the European Foundation for the Improvement of Living and Working Conditions found that EU workers were under much greater time pressure than a decade ago. A third now spends all or almost all of their time rushing to meet deadlines. Of course, speed has a role in the workplace. A deadline can focus the mind and spur us on to perform remarkable feats. The trouble is that many of us are permanently stuck in deadline mode, leaving little time to ease off and recharge. The things that need slowness—strategic planning, creative thought, building relationships—get lost in the mad dash to keep up, or even just to look busy.

Erwin Heller, a member of the Society for the Deceleration of Time, enjoys the benefits of working more slowly at his law firm in Munich. Like many attorneys, he used to rush through get-to-know meetings with clients—ten minutes to suss out the brief and then straight down to tackling the case. After a while, though, he noticed that he was always placing follow-up calls to clients, and would sometimes set off in the wrong direction and have to backtrack. "Most people come to lawyers with goals that they tell you about, like money, and goals that they don't, like being acknowledged or getting justice or revenge," he says.

—
Instead of using Blackberrys, laptops and cell phones to extend the workday, we can use them to rearrange it.

"It takes time to get through to the hidden wishes that motivate clients, but you have to know these to do the best job for them." These days, his initial meetings last up to two hours, during which he develops a thorough grasp of the client's personality, circumstances, values, aims and fears. As a result, Heller, a lively 56-year-old with a goatee and a mischievous grin, works more efficiently, and his business is booming. "Clients are always telling me that with other lawyers you get five minutes to explain what you need, you hand over the papers and you're out the door," he says. "Though it may seem very slow and old-fashioned, listening is the best policy. The worst thing is to rush into action."

Many companies are now trying to strike a balance between fast and slow at work. Often this means recognizing the limits of technology. Email, for all its speed, cannot capture irony, nuance or body language, and this leads to misunderstandings and mistakes. Slower methods of communication—walking across the office and actually talking to someone face-to-face, for instance—can save time and money, and build esprit de corps, in the long run. That is one reason that companies have started urging staff to think hard before they hit the send button. In 2001, Nestlé Rowntree became the first of many UK firms to introduce email-free Fridays. A year later, British Airways ran a series of TV commercials with a "slower is better" theme. In one, a group of businessmen think they've won an order from a US firm by faxing across a proposal. Their rivals end up stealing the deal by taking the time to fly over and make the pitch face-to-face.

Companies are also moving to make work less of a 24/7 treadmill. The accountancy firm Ernst & Young recently told its US employees that it was okay not to check email and voice mail over the weekend. In a similar vein, stressed-out executives are taking the heretical step of turning off their cell phones outside the office. Jill Hancock, a go-getting investment banker in London, used to take her chic, chrome-plated Nokia everywhere, and even answered calls on vacation or in the middle of a romantic dinner. She paid the price, though, in depression and chronic fatigue. When a psychologist diagnosed "mobile phone addiction" and urged her to switch off from time to time, Hancock was appalled. But eventually she gave it a try, first silencing the Nokia during her lunch break, and later on evenings and weekend when an urgent call was unlikely. Within two months, she was off the antidepressants, her skin had cleared up and she was getting more work done in less time. At the bank, her colleagues accept that Hancock is no longer reachable around the clock. A few have even followed her example. "I didn't realize it at the time, but the fact that I was always available, always on, was grinding me down," she says. "We all need time to ourselves." Decelerating at work also prompted Hancock to make more room for Slow pursuits in the rest of her life. She has taken up yoga and now cooks a real supper, instead of a microwaved meal, at least two evenings a week.

To avoid burnout, and to promote creative thinking, business gurus, therapists and psychologists increasingly prescribe doses of slowness for the workplace. In his best-selling 2002 book, *How to Succeed in Business Without Working So Damn Hard*, Robert Kriegel suggested taking regular 15- to 20-minute time-outs during the day. Dr. Donald Hensrud, director of the Mayo Clinic Executive Health Program, advises, "Try shutting your office door and closing your eyes for 15 minutes. Lean back and breathe deeply."

Even in high-speed, high-pressure industries, companies are taking steps to help their staff slow down. Some grant sabbaticals in hopes that an extended period away from the office will refresh employees and stir their creative juices. Others offer on-the-job yoga, aromatherapy and massage, or encourage workers to eat lunch away from their desks. Some firms have installed chill-out rooms. At the Tokyo office of Oracle, the software giant, the staff has access to a soundproof meditation room with a wooden floor bordered by smooth pebbles and Oriental objets d'art.

—
Many modern jobs depend on the kind of creative thinking that seldom occurs at a desk and cannot be squeezed into fixed schedules.

The room's lighting is soft, and a hint of incense hangs in the air. At the flick of a switch, the soothing sounds of a babbling brook tinkle from the stereo system.

Takeshi Sato is a big fan of the eighth-floor sanctuary. As manager of the CEO's office, he works a 12-hour day, juggling emails, meetings, phone calls and budget reports. When the pace becomes too frenetic, he leaves his desk to spend ten minutes in the meditation room. "At times in the day, I suddenly feel like I need to be slow, to relax, to let my mind become still and quiet," he tells me. "Some people might think of that as ten minutes of lost time, but I see it as ten minutes well invested. It's very important for performance to be able to switch on and off, between fast and slow. After I have been in the meditation room, my mind is sharper and calmer, which helps me make good decisions."

Other people are taking deceleration to its ultimate conclusion and actually catching 40 winks during the working day. Though sleeping on the job is the ultimate taboo, research has shown that a short "power nap"—around 20 minutes is ideal—can boost energy and productivity. A recent study by NASA concluded that 24 minutes of shut-eye did wonders for a pilot's alertness and performance. Many of the most vigorous and successful figures in history were inveterate nappers: John F. Kennedy, Thomas Edison, Napoleon Bonaparte, John D. Rockefeller, Johannes Brahms. Winston Churchill delivered the most eloquent defense of the afternoon snooze: "Don't think you will be doing less work because you sleep during the day. That's a foolish notion helped by people who have no imagination. You will be able to accomplish more. You get two days in one—well, at least one and a half."

Napping can be especially helpful nowadays, when so many of us are not sleeping enough at night. Backed by pro-sleep groups such as the World Napping Organization to the Portuguese Association of Friends of the Siesta, snoozing in the middle of the workday is enjoying a renaissance. At its six factories in the US, Yarde Metals en-

courages staff to doze during breaks. The company has built special "nap rooms" and once a year holds a collective napping session complete with buffet lunch and silly costumes. Vechta, a small city in northern Germany, urges its civil servants to take a postprandial snooze in their office chairs or at home. From the American factory floor to the German town hall, the results are the same: happier staff, better morale, higher productivity. More on-the-job napping may be in the pipeline. In 2001, Sedus, a leading European manufacturer of office furniture, unveiled a new chair that opens up to a horizontal position to allow people to catch a few ZZZs at their desks.

In Spain, meanwhile, the siesta is coming back with a modern twist. Since most Spaniards no longer have time to go home at lunch for a big meal and a nap, *Masajes a 1000* (Massages for 1000), a nationwide network of "siesta salons" now offers everyone from bankers to bartenders the chance to grab 20 minutes of sleep for four euros.

At the branch in Barcelona's Mallorca Street, every detail is designed to relax. The walls are painted a soothing shade of peach, and the rooms are warm and softly lit. New Age music whispers from hidden speakers. Fully clothed and kneeling face-down in ergonomically designed chairs, the customers enjoy head, neck and back massages. Once customers drift off to sleep, the masseur drapes a thick woolen blanket over them and moves on. As I settle into my chair, at least three people in the room are snoring gently. A couple of minutes later, I join them.

Afterward, on the sidewalk outside, I fall into conversation with a young salesman called Luis, who is straightening his tie after a 15-minute snooze. He looks as refreshed as I feel. "This is so much better than going to the gym," he says, snapping his briefcase shut. "I feel totally energized. I feel ready for anything."

To let work take over our lives is folly. There are too many important things that need time, such as friends, family, hobbies and rest.

AN INTERVIEW WITH CARL HONORÉ

*Carl Honoré is one of the world's most respected advocates of
the Slow movement—not just slow food, but also work, communication
and life. Eleven years after publishing his standout tome* In Praise of Slowness
*(the chapter "Work: The Benefits of Working Less Hard" was excerpted in the
previous pages), he offers some insight on what Slow means today.*

HOW IS WORKING MORE SLOWLY OFTEN ACTUALLY
MORE PRODUCTIVE THAN WORKING QUICKLY?
In lots of ways. You can only squeeze so much productivity out of a human being. Eventually people burn out or lose interest, but working too hard and too fast takes a toll from the very start. Staffers become less creative and more error-prone. A long-hours work culture also leads to a lot of wasted time as employees hang around pretending to be busy when all they're doing is putting in face time.

Study after study has shown that time pressure is only useful up to a certain point. Beyond that, it takes a toll. When people feel too rushed and are constantly working with one eye on the clock, they become less creative. Instead of coming up with bold, innovative ideas, they go for the low-hanging fruit. That is why forward-thinking companies are looking for ways to help their staff slow down. Some are giving employees more control over their schedules so they can work at their own pace, slowing down and speeding up when it suits them. Others are capping work hours. Even Wall Street banks have taken steps in this direction in recent months.

Many firms are encouraging staff to shift into a lower gear during the workday. That means creating quiet spaces where employees can do yoga, pray, get a massage or even take a short nap. The boom in meditation and mindfulness programs in the corporate world is another sign that business is waking up to the power of slowing down. Meditation lowers stress, enhances feelings of calm and sharpens concentration. Over time, it also re-wires the brain so that it can process information faster.

A perfect illustration of the best way to thrive in a fast world is not to go faster and faster, but to slow down.

HOW HAS THE RECESSION AFFECTED OUR WORK
AND OUR OFFICE ENVIRONMENTS?
On one hand, the recession has accelerated many workplaces. Belt-tightening and downsizing have put more pressure on remaining staff to do more and more in less and less time. And in a culture that still places a premium on speed and busyness, people feel that a good way to appear indispensable is to give the impression of constant rushing and activity. As in: "I must be hugely important and productive because I'm always busy."

On the other hand, the recession is a jolting reminder that the way we have been living is unsustainable. The pursuit of fast growth, fast profits and fast consumption has brought the world to its knees. It has made us unhappy and unhealthy. People are yearning for an alternative. More and more of us are coming around to the idea that we need to reinvent the way we run our economies and societies from the ground up. Slowing down will be a big part of that change.

On the other side of the equation, the recession may prove to be a boon to Slow outside the workplace. When people have less money to throw around, they are more likely to embrace slower forms of leisure such as walking, cycling, conversation and playing board games. That may explain why home cooking has surged in the US. It may start as a grudging act of self-denial, but eventually people realize that slower forms of leisure can actually be fun, nourishing and relaxing.

IS THERE ANY WAY THAT TECHNOLOGY CAN HELP US SLOW DOWN INSTEAD OF SPEEDING US UP?

Absolutely. People often assume that, as a proponent of the Slow movement, I must be against new technology. They assume slowing down means throwing away the gadgets, yet nothing could be further from the truth. I am no Luddite: I love technology and own all the latest high-tech goodies. To me, being able to speak and write to anyone, anytime, anywhere is exhilarating. By freeing us from the constraints of time and space, mobile communication can help us seize the moment, which is the ultimate aim of Slow.

But there are limits. The truth is that communicating more does not always mean communicating better. You see parents staring at smartphones while spending "quality time" with their children. Surveys suggest that a fifth of us now interrupt sex to read an email or answer a call. Is that seizing the moment, or wasting it?

Whenever a new technology comes along, it takes time to work out how to get the most from it. Mobile communication is no exception: It's neither good nor bad—what matters is how we use it. The challenge is to use communication technology more wisely. To switch on when it brings us together and enriches our lives, but to switch off when old-fashioned, face-to-face communication—or even just a little silence—is called for.

Human beings need moments of silence and solitude—to rest and recharge; to think deeply and creatively; to look inside and confront the big questions: Who am I? How do I fit into the world? What is the meaning of life? Being "always on" militates against all of that. You cannot daydream or reflect when your mind is constantly wondering if you have a new text message or if it's time for a fresh tweet.

The bottom line is that technology can help us slow down if we deploy it judiciously. That means using it to get things done efficiently and thereby save time—but then switching it off so we don't waste that saved time by being constantly distracted. We also have to dedicate that saved time to Slow pursuits rather than simply cramming it with more work or consumption.

FOR THOSE WHO ARE IN CONTROL OF THEIR OWN TIME, HOW CAN FULL-TIME FREELANCERS LEARN TO DIVIDE THEIR WORK AND SOCIAL LIVES?

It's both essential and possible to do. If you never stop working, then you never recharge your batteries or allow your mind to slip into the creative mode of thought that psychologists call "slow thinking." Most of us know when enough is enough: You feel yourself flagging physically.

You need a coffee or a Red Bull to keep going. Your concentration starts to wander. You find yourself needing to go over things several times to take them in. Everything takes longer than it should. You start to lose your temper more easily. The joy drains away and everything feels like a chore. Detach it by setting aside fixed times for working and for not working, taking a hard look at how much time new projects will take before accepting them, booking time to switch off the gadgets, creating a separate physical space (home office, library, café, corner of the living room, etc.) for working and pinning up reminders in that space such as holiday snaps or children's artwork of why it's important to put down your tools.

WHAT IS THE BIGGEST FORCE THAT PREVENTS US FROM ALL LIVING SLOWER LIVES?

Fear: fear of failure, of scorn, of missing out and the fear of being alone with ourselves.

FRANCE IS FREQUENTLY USED AS AN EXAMPLE IN YOUR BOOK. HOW HAS THE COUNTRY CHANGED FROM ITS HARD STANCE IN THE PAST DECADE?

France's famous 35-hour workweek was always going to run into trouble because it was a top-down, one-size-fits-all remedy. It was too inflexible. And there are limits to how far legislation can remake the world. Over the past decade, the 35-hour week has become more of a symbol or an aspiration than a reality in that country. Successive governments have watered it down and both companies and their workers have found ways around the law. Today, French workers put in 39.5 hours per week on average, which is just fractionally below the European average.

WHAT OTHER COUNTRIES ARE APPROACHING WORK-LIFE BALANCE IN AN INTERESTING WAY?

Germany is a shining example at the moment—its economy is a powerhouse of productivity, and yet Germans work far fewer hours than citizens of most other countries. When they're at work, they focus—checking Facebook is verboten—and get a lot done. And when they're away from work, they leave the office behind and focus on friends, family and leisure pursuits. They also put up a firewall between work and private life: Leading German firms such as Volkswagen, Puma and BMW have stopped staff from sending or receiving email outside working hours. The German Ministry of Labor has done the same, and has banned managers from contacting staff at home except in emergencies.

> "People worry about missing out on life if they slow down, but life is what's happening right here, right now."

ANOTHER NATION THAT PRAISES SLOW ACTIVITIES SUCH AS TEA CEREMONIES AND BONSAI IS JAPAN, YET THEY HAVE SOME OF THE MOST NOTORIOUS WORK HOURS IN THE WORLD. WHAT DO THESE INCONSISTENCIES SAY ABOUT OUR CULTURES?

No culture gets it all right. The Italians are masters of Slow Food, but if you've ever driven on a highway in Italy, you know the Italians are not immune to the virus of hurry. Every culture has traditions and rituals for slowing down—human beings couldn't survive without them—but we all get infected by the worldwide pressure to speed up. You can find people overworking in every culture, but it does seem that some cultures are more prone to logging long hours.

IS THERE A GENERATIONAL ASPECT TO THIS DEBATE? ARE MILLENNIALS ACTUALLY MORE LIKELY TO BE HAPPY WORKERS THAN THEIR OVERWORKED, CLOSE-TO-RETIREMENT BABY-BOOMER PARENTS?

The pressure for Slow is coming from all age groups. Boomers, for instance, are reaching an age when they no longer have the energy to do 100-hour weeks and are eager to slow down and savor the time they have left. Millennials are coming of age with a very different set of priorities. They're looking at the older generations and recoiling: They don't want to sacrifice their health, relationships, dreams and souls to achieve what now seems like an outdated notion of success. They don't want to work for companies that plunder the environment or behave unethically. Sure, they want to do well, but they also want to do good. And that is the Slow movement in a nutshell. Millennials love their social media but are increasingly waking up to the fact that being always on and constantly distracted is hampering their ability to think, enjoy the moment and connect deeply with other people. So they're coming up with innovative ways to switch off. One example is "stacking": When some people go out for a meal, everyone places their phones in a stack in the middle of the table, and the first person to reach for a device pays the bill for the whole table.

It's a delightful way to put a speed limit on the information superhighway in order to keep everyone in the moment together.

HOW CAN WE LEARN TO ALLOW OURSELVES TO LEAVE WORK AT 5 P.M. WITHOUT GUILT OR ANXIETY?

It's tough to do this alone. To vanquish the taboo against slowing down, we need to open up a conversation with our colleagues to make the benefits of not being chained to work clear. It also helps to read and share the mountain of research showing that overwork is the enemy of efficiency, productivity and creativity. We all need to be more open and honest about the benefits of clocking off early—otherwise the macho culture of working long hours will always hold the upper hand.

A LOT OF PEOPLE FEEL LIKE THEY DON'T HAVE THE TIME TO BE SLOW. WHAT STEPS CAN WE TAKE TOWARD A SLOWER LIFE?

My response would be that if you don't have the time to be slow, then you aren't really living properly. You're racing through life instead of living it. People worry about missing out on life if they slow down, but life is what's happening right here, right now. As for steps to lead a slower life: Do less. Buy less. Consume less. Drive less. Unplug more. Walk more. Sleep more. Stop multitasking and do one thing at a time. Embed slow moments and rituals into your schedule.

FOR THOSE WORKING IN A CORPORATE CULTURE WHERE THE IDEA OF FLEXIBILITY IS CHOOSING WHEN YOU TAKE YOUR LUNCH BREAK, IS IT POSSIBLE TO INSTILL A SLOWER WORK LIFESTYLE AMID AN UN-SLOW REGIME?

It's obviously hard to slow down in a company that denigrates slowness. But there are two ways to fight back: First, commit small acts of rebellion whenever possible. At your workstation, do one thing at time instead of falling into the multitasking trap—you'll get more done in less time and feel less harried. Switch off email

> "I don't really have a mantra, but I do often remind myself who won the race between the tortoise and the hare."

notifications and only look at your in-box at fixed times rather than allowing incoming messages to distract you constantly. Get up from your workstation and go for a short walk once every hour. When you feel flustered and over-rushed, take a few deep breaths. And secondly, start tackling the company culture.

HOW WOULD YOU RECOMMEND EMPLOYEES PRESENT THESE IDEAS TO THEIR BOSSES, *INCEPTION*-STYLE?
Slowly! You need to win them over gradually. First you have to provide the evidence that many high-flying companies are putting Slow into action and reaping the benefits. Then try to meet to discuss ways you could all slow down productively, or suggest a trial week of slow practices—nothing beats slow in action.

WHAT HAVE BEEN YOUR FAVORITE PROJECTS THAT YOU'VE WORKED ON IN THE PAST DECADE?
I've really enjoyed being a booster and mentor for other people who are putting Slow into action, whether it's with Slow Art, Slow Work, Slow Education, Slow Fashion, Slow Reading, Slow Food, Slow Travel and so on. There are so many micro movements for different aspects of Slow out there and it's thrilling to know I've had a hand in many of them. I made a program for BBC Radio 4 in the UK where I helped three people slow down. It was a challenge taking my ideas from the page and putting them into the real world, but it worked and was lots of fun. Now I'm making a TV show for the ABC in Australia where I'm attempting to slow down three frazzled families, which is an even bigger challenge because there are so many more pieces to the puzzle when you bring children into the equation. But it's thrilling and gratifying when you see people learning to love Slow.

YOU'RE AN INCREDIBLY BUSY MAN WHO HARDLY SEEMS LIKE HE COULD LIVE THE SLOW LIFE! CAN YOU BE BOTH BUSY AND SLOW?
It may look like that from the outside but I assure you it doesn't feel that way! I'm living at a pace that works for me. When I'm on, I'm on. But I make sure to be off a lot of the time too. I don't work evenings or weekends and I always take lots of holidays. Yes, you can be busy and slow, but only if you have the right amount of busy. Slow is about relearning the lost art of shifting gears, of moving from moments of busyness to moments of slowness. If you get the right balance, it can work wonders.

HAVE YOU EVER STRUGGLED TO PRACTICE WHAT YOU PREACH?
The only time I feel like I might be falling off the wagon is when I lose control of my own schedule. This doesn't happen very often because I'm my own boss, but when it does, I'm much better at rolling with the punches than I was before. Because I live most of my life at my own pace, I'm better able to cope with the stresses and strains that arise when things start moving too fast. I don't get affected by other people's stress or impatience. I keep my head while everyone around me is losing theirs. People are always telling me I'm surprisingly calm and unflustered, so it must be working!

WHAT PERSONAL RULES DO YOU ABIDE BY?
I keep a tight rein on my use of technology. To avoid getting overloaded, I turn down a lot of work offers, including some I'd have cut off a leg to do ten years ago. During the day I conduct random speed audits, stopping from time to time to make sure I'm not going too fast. I don't really have a mantra, but I do often remind myself who won the race between the tortoise and the hare.

HOW CAN WE CHANGE THE GLOBAL CONSCIOUSNESS TOWARD SLOW? WHERE DO WE NEED TO START?
We need to start with ourselves. As Gandhi said, "You need to be the change you want to see in the world." That means we have to set an example by embracing Slow in our own lives and then shouting it from the rooftops.

TO LEARN MORE, VISIT CARLHONORE.COM

WORDS
JAMES CARTWRIGHT

PHOTOGRAPHS
PELLE CREPIN

STYLING
ARADIA CROCKETT

The Path to Success

Our career paths can be filled with plenty of unexpected detours, speed bumps and potholes, and it isn't always easy to decide which route to take. Sometimes it's best to enjoy the road you're on as you confidently stride into uncharted territory.

"I shall be telling this with a sigh
Somewhere ages and ages hence:
Two roads diverged in a wood, and I—
I took the one less traveled by,
And that has made all the difference."
— the final stanza of Robert Frost's "The Road Not Taken"

This Robert Frost poem is often used as a happy-go-lucky rally to follow your own path and forge ahead without heeding the consequences. But compared with the instant success stories we hear through the internet's grapevine, Frost's invitation to carpe diem willy-nilly can sometimes appear naive. The entrepreneurial lore that's repeated in countless self-help books doesn't often talk about the paths that sent us veering off-track or lead to nowhere, and the people we look up to may have ironed out the bumps in their roads, crediting their achievements to twists of fate and chance occurrences. If you add those bumps back in, you may get a clearer picture of the often-circuitous routes to success.

The characters in the greatest entrepreneurial success stories are just as capable of losing their way as the rest of us. For every Zuckerberg or Jobs—with their motivated movie-ready backstories—there have been thousands of talented visionaries who wandered down Frost's less-traveled path before finding their feet again.

Take Walt Disney, the architect of generations of childhood dreams: He was once fired from his job in journalism for lacking imagination and ideas. When he did finally pull one out of the bag—a giant cartoon mouse—he was told that his character would be frightening to women. And there are others: Madonna had a stint working at Dunkin' Donuts before going on to become the most successful recording artist of her time; Albert Einstein was a slow starter, unable to speak for the first four years of his life; and then there's J.K. Rowling, Elvis Presley, Anna Wintour and Thomas Edison, all of whom were known to have gone through wilderness years.

Others have come across their ways accidentally while on quite a different path. Yvon Chouinard now presides over one of the most esteemed outdoor clothing brands in the world, Patagonia, but his route wasn't exactly direct. In 1953, an adolescent Yvon was immersed in a local falcony club, teaching his hawks to hunt for prey while he rappeled down cliffs. Dissatisfied with the gear out there, he taught himself the skills required to fabricate his own climbing equipment and began producing pitons to sell to his fellow climbers. It took a long time for him to find the sweet spot of his unintended commercial venture, and legend has it he even ate cat food to survive the tougher times. Looking at Patagonia today, it seems unthinkable that the revered clothing brand wasn't meticulously planned—that its success was born out of a dangerous pastime and pure good fortune.

When we're standing at the fork in the road, what's important to grasp is that the road doesn't matter. Whether the one less traveled or the one well-trodden, there's no way to really know what kind of journey we're choosing. Since we'll never be able to walk that second road and know where it led, we may as well enjoy the one we're on.

WORDS
SAMMI MASSEY

PHOTOGRAPHS
JONAS BJERRE-POULSEN

A Sense
of Spaces

*Paying attention to the five senses can help your visitors feel at home,
whether you work in an office, run a café or have your own store. We asked
architect, designer and photographer Jonas Bjerre-Poulsen to take us on
a tour of Copenhagen spaces that get the experience just right.*

↓ Couches upholstered in Hallingdal wool absorb unwanted sounds to create a shielded and cozy setting.

↓ This table references Kvadrat's industrial neighborhood while their signature wall-mounted Clouds offer acoustic privacy.

SOUND

Danish textile maker Kvadrat has put a great deal of thought, time and research into finding a good balance when it comes to acoustics. Soft materials can dampen the clattery noise that often comes with a minimal and uncluttered space.

Mastering the art of shaping the sound in your space can help draw in your patrons whether you're selling attire, displaying art or serving up refreshments. Tania Christensen, the PR manager at Danish textile maker Kvadrat, emphasizes the importance of differentiating between "sound" and "noise": "*Noise* is by definition a distraction that is irritating and unwanted," she says. "*Sound* is created with meaning and can enhance the perception of particular visual sets of information." The goal is to limit noise while creating a harmony of desirable sounds such as conversation, music and natural ambience. Modern and minimal spaces can be beautiful but present challenges when creating a warm sound profile. "The trend is to be as minimalistic as possible with a lot of hard surfaces and open-plan spaces," she says. "Although this aesthetic looks great, it creates a lot of acoustic problems as sounds keep vibrating and create *noise*, which makes it hard for people to concentrate and communicate." Fortunately, there are simple ways that shops, galleries and offices can foster softer acoustics without sacrificing elegance. Textiles are highly effective for decreasing unwanted noise as they absorb echoes and other harsh or distracting dins: Try fabrics such as curtains, rugs, upholsteries or Soft Cells (Kvadrat's textile panels). Playing soft music can also help to soften the harsh edges of footsteps and echoes. Balancing the acoustics is a powerful way to keep your customers calm and engaged. "Visual perception of space is on the conscious level, whereas the audible perception is almost entirely on the subconscious level, which is why it's such a strong tool," Tania says.

↓ Outdoor landscapes were the inspiration for the design at Verandah. These long curtains recall the color of sky and water.

↓ Soft, comfortable pillows complement the monochromatic interior of this popular restaurant while also absorbing noise.

TOUCH

The folks at Danish restaurant Verandah explain how they use textiles and textures to make their space feel more welcoming and give their diners a more comfortable communal seating arrangement.

Enhancing the tactile dimensions of your space can up the ante of the guest experience. More than simply making things plush and supple, it's important to foster a variety of surfaces that contrast and complement each other. A little wood here, a little metal there, a touch of thick cotton—that's how Verandah approaches interior surfaces. "Just as you'd see many different shapes and tones outside, you would also see those in Verandah," says marketing manager Bryndal Bennett. The space proves that interiors inspired by exterior spaces can feel more natural and cozy. Verandah takes inspiration from the outside living rooms of traditional Indian homes and fuses that with the Danish love of minimalism. "The colors are similar to the outdoors but with design accents that reflect the Indian veranda," she says. Try incorporating a range of textures from your environment into your shop or office through rustic colors and natural materials such as salvaged woods and stone. Instead of the usual hard upright chairs used in most modern restaurants, Verandah gives their clientele a comfier experience. Mixing up communal seating—couches, benches and love seats—with individual chairs encourages more meaningful encounters. This helps guests view dining as a familial affair, no matter the group size: "Larger tables allow for a more convivial experience, whereas the smaller tables provide a sense of intimacy," she says. Lastly, never underestimate the power of comfort, and remember not to sacrifice it to the gods of minimalism while striking what Bryndal describes as "the perfect balance between having a sleek modern look but using fabrics and furniture that entice you to stay longer."

↓ The Humphrey lamp by Kevin Josias: "I like the simplicity of the design combined with the fact you can turn the metal circle."

↓ These long linen rust-colored curtains are from Studio Oliver Gustav. The iron bar and hooks are custom-made by a local designer.

↓ Yvonne Koné has found that dusty pink walls add a feminine touch to her simple and clean designs.

SIGHT

Fashion designer Yvonne Koné talks about the importance of light, space and making sure nothing comes between your customer and the products. Incorporating everything from soft natural light to gentle paint colors enhances her shop's interior.

The appearance of a space can either gently beckon shoppers or frighten them off. Thankfully, the path to a visually balanced space has already been paved by experts such as Yvonne Koné, an accessory, bag and shoe designer whose space epitomizes the delicate balance between warmth and beauty that we all hope to achieve in our shops and offices. The first principle to crafting a space that soothes weary eyes is to note that natural lighting is always better: Yvonne lets in as much sunlight as possible through her windows and avoids pitting artificial light sources against natural light. This is easy enough during long summer days, but there are also ways to keep your customers and guests well-lit during winter without the need to crank up the fluorescents. "I often suggest that clients go outside to see the products in natural daylight," she says. Yvonne also brings in smaller lamps with soft light—this helps the space glow so passersby know it's open. Layout is the next thing to consider in grooming the appearance of your space. "The goal is to make a simple yet personal space that complements the products," she says. "Cleanliness and a lack of clutter help visitors focus on what's important, whether it's the communal table or the products." She sees minimalism as transparency—the goal is to make sure that nothing stands in the way between people and the contents. The final step is your personal touch, which separates minimalism from sterility: Plants, fabrics and paint colors will make your space feel like home to anyone who stops in. "If a shop isn't in harmony with the products, it can be really difficult to sell anything," she says.

↓
Oliver Gustav uses a variety of natural scents such as flowers and essential oils to help create a more dynamic envrionment.

↓
Organic Mad et Len candles that contain custom-blended scents are encased in handmade wrought steel.

SCENT

Creative consultant Oliver Gustav combines all kinds of natural scents into his aesthetic environment. He uses plants, flowers, candles and even potpourri in order to freshen his rooms and keep his spaces feeling airy.

A pleasant scent should be part of the dynamic world of sensation. Oliver Gustav uses natural sources to keep his studio and showroom smelling wonderful: "I don't avoid having contrasting scents together. They seem to make room for each other," he says, noting that his fragrances complement each other because they're delicate and natural. He's adept at integrating smells into what he calls the "aesthetic universe" of his studio— beautiful objects on display, music and natural fragrance are woven together through their simplicity and elegant placement. Oliver places candles throughout his shop and prefers those in metal containers to limit the risk of fire. While lighting candles, he enjoys simultaneously keeping a potpourri going in order to build up layers of delicate smell: "I always have a potpourri on either resin or lava stone with scented oil on top in the room," he says. Plants and flowers bring both aesthetic and olfactory goodness to a room. Oliver says he likes "all kinds of different types of geraniums, and picking out blue hyacinths and placing them in a big jar." By favoring biological sources of good smells, the aroma will evolve with the seasons and reflect your region: The most effective sources are natural purifiers such as beeswax candles and plants. As for keeping tricky areas such as the bathroom and kitchen smelling nice, remember not to try too hard with artificial fragrances or heavily scented candles—if these spaces are kept clean, a pleasant plant and a few spritzes of essential oil spray will keep the air fresh. Overall, your space should smell as you wish it to. "Smells make a big impression on me and they sort of dictate a mood in my rooms," he says.

TASTE

Garde Hvalsøe is a bespoke kitchen and cabinet maker that shares all kinds of edible goodies with their clients—often neatly arranged in custom-made drawers—as a way to enrich the customer experience.

Inviting flavors are not just for restaurants and bakeries: Non-food shops and workplaces may also incorporate a delicious touch into their repertoire in order to commune with customers and coworkers to make them feel more at ease. Søren Lundh Aagaard, co-owner of Garde Hvalsøe, says: "We are foodies so we often have wild boar or some other interesting food available for our clients. This not only pleases their eyes but their taste buds as well." The company sets an example by bringing food into the unexpected realm of home design, reminding us that sharing meals and snacks often leads to friendlier connections. Sometimes this might mean leaving a tray of cookies out on the counter, selling your baker friend's confections or setting out a bowl of taffy in your meeting room. But in addition to tasty giveaways, there are deeper ways to connect with others through the channel of taste. Any type of shop can bend the rules and hold an unexpected family-style meal to celebrate a new season or milestone. If you don't have a kitchen fit for making a large meal, you could also follow Garde Hvalsøe's lead and team up with a local restaurant or caterer: The team provides meals for its potential clients from a local eatery called I'm a Kombo. Sharing meals with clients is a way to get to know their needs more deeply than you ever would over the phone or in the office. Finally, when it comes to enjoying meals with others, remember to keep it simple and let the food speak for itself. "Less is definitely more—try to make sure the focus is on the raw ingredients," Søren says. Food is an effective ingredient that always helps to enliven those human connections.

ESSAY
LIZ CLAYTON

RECIPES
DIANA YEN

PHOTOGRAPHS
GENTL & HYERS

Caffeine à la Carte

Do you need more coffee in your life beyond your morning mug and afternoon pick-me-up? Designed with budding entrepreneurs in mind, the following pages' recipes will give you inspiration for other ways to fulfill your daily caffeine consumption.

Everything in your life can be coffee if you really want it to be. It just makes sense. Coffee, and its ability to somehow soothe and vivify at the same time, provides a through-line in so many of our lives. From unconsciousness into morning, it sparks creativity at work and later revitalizes us for the playtime that comes after. So why limit its gifts to those of imbibement? Coffee, whether it's in your body, on your body or simply near it, can surround you with its comfort in so very many ways.

Beyond merely drinking this magical elixir, there are myriad ways to consume it. In fact, coffee was originally eaten rather than brewed. According to ancient legend, there was a goatherd named Kaldi whose dancing, leaping charges revealed that the source of their jubilation was grazing on the fruits of the wild coffee bushes of Ethiopia. In modern times, we've figured out a more bingeable, chocolate-enrobed version of this stimulant, and infusing food with coffee has only become more elegant as chefs learn more about the subtlety and variation of roasts and origins. It's a natural fit in beer: The sweet deep tones of a sultry roasted coffee can be perfectly suited to the palates of porters or chocolatey stouts. Ground espresso has found its way into spice mixes for delectable meat rubs, combining beautifully with ingredients such as cocoa, Tellicherry pepper and sumac. Coffee and cheese also make surprisingly friendly bedfellows (you'll find it in aromatic rinds and other mysterious places), and let's not forget the supreme expression of coffee in any proximity to ice cream.

Coffee can be all around you in the home too. You can put it on your furniture—on purpose, even—as a gentle-tinted wood stain, or apply it with a small brush or swab as a scratch cover. Spent coffee grounds can clean and scrub your pots and pans, and what's more, they can do the same for your skin: Moistened coffee grounds either used on their own as a skin exfoliant or incorporated into lotions as part of a stimulating coffee massage therapy treatment are credited with stimulating circulation and transmitting their antioxidant benefits to the skin. It also has heaps of beneficial uses in the garden from general-purpose composting to intentionally rebalancing your soil's acidity. Want to change the color of your hydrangeas? Coffee grounds are here to help you go from white to blue.

And if coffee has awakened your artistic side after all that cooking, gardening and spa therapy, anything leftover in the pot makes a lovely watercolor-like paint. It's a classic aid in creating an antique effect on paper—just remember, would-be historic-document forgers, that your papers will smell revealingly, deliciously like what you've been brewing all along.

ROASTED BABY BEETS WITH COFFEE-BALSAMIC GLAZE

By marrying two of our favorite ingredients, this appetizer offers roasted beets with a gentle coffee glaze that is both flavorful and intriguing.

3 pounds (1.4 kilograms) mixed baby red and golden
  beets, trimmed, scrubbed and halved
2 tablespoons extra-virgin olive oil
2 tablespoons unsalted butter, melted
Salt and freshly ground pepper
½ cup (120 milliliters) brewed light- to medium-roast coffee
½ cup (120 milliliters) balsamic vinegar
2 tablespoons honey
One 3-inch (7.5-centimeter) strip of orange peel
½ cup (100 grams) crumbled goat cheese
¼ cup (30 grams) chopped roasted walnuts
1 tablespoon chopped fresh dill

Preheat the oven to 400°F (200°C). In a large bowl, toss the beets with the olive oil and butter and season them generously with salt and pepper. Place the beets on a rimmed baking sheet and cover tightly with foil. Roast until fork tender, 20 to 30 minutes. Cool to room temperature.

Meanwhile, in a medium saucepan, combine the coffee, vinegar, honey and orange peel. Bring the mixture to a boil over medium-high heat, stirring to dissolve the honey. Continue to boil until the glaze is a syrup consistency and is reduced to ⅓ cup, 8 to 10 minutes. Discard the orange peel and set the glaze aside to cool.

Arrange the beets on a platter and drizzle with the glaze. Garnish with the goat cheese, walnuts and dill.

ESPRESSO-CHILI RUBBED STEAK WITH HERB SALAD

This full-flavored rub is made with espresso beans, chili powder, paprika and other ingredients that give the steak a spicy-sweet taste.

FOR THE ESPRESSO-CHILI RUB

2 tablespoons finely ground Italian
   espresso beans

2 tablespoons ancho or chipotle chili powder

1 tablespoon light brown sugar

1 tablespoon Spanish paprika

1 ½ teaspoons kosher salt, plus more
   for sprinkling

½ teaspoon freshly ground pepper

Pinch of cinnamon

FOR THE STEAK

3 thick-cut steaks, such as rib eye, New York
   strip or sirloin (3 to 3 ½ pounds/1.4 to 1.6
   kilograms total), cut 1 ¼-inch (3-centimeters)
   thick, at room temperature

Salt and freshly ground pepper

2 tablespoons vegetable oil

FOR THE SALAD

¼ cup (60 milliliters) fresh lemon juice

1 tablespoon Dijon mustard

1 garlic clove, minced

½ teaspoon salt

¼ teaspoon freshly ground pepper

½ cup (120 milliliters) extra-virgin olive oil

7 cups (170 grams) loosely packed mesclun greens

¼ cup (5 grams) loosely packed fresh tarragon leaves

¼ cup (5 grams) loosely packed fresh
   flat-leaf parsley leaves

¼ cup (5 grams) loosely packed fresh dill sprigs

¼ cup (5 grams) loosely packed fresh mint leaves

ESPRESSO-CHILI RUB

In a small bowl, mix together the espresso, chili powder, brown sugar, paprika, salt, pepper and cinnamon. The rub will keep in an airtight container at room temperature for several months.

STEAK

About 30 minutes before cooking, pat the steaks dry and season them generously with salt and pepper. Sprinkle with about 2 tablespoons of the rub and pat to coat all sides. Set the steaks aside to come to room temperature. Preheat the oven to 350°F (180°C).

   Heat 2 large skillets, preferably cast-iron, over medium-high heat. Add 1 table-spoon of oil to each pan. When the oil begins to smoke, add the steaks and cook until dark brown and crusted and an instant-read thermometer inserted into the center of each one registers 120°F (48°C) for medium-rare, or 125°F (52°C) for medium, 3 to 5 minutes per side. Remove the steaks from the heat and transfer them to a cutting board to rest before serving, about 5 minutes.

SALAD

In a small bowl, whisk together the lemon juice, mustard, garlic, salt and pepper. Continue to whisk while adding the olive oil in a slow, steady stream to emulsify the dressing. In a large bowl, toss together the greens, herbs and just enough of the dressing to lightly coat.

   Slice the steaks and fan them on a platter. Serve immediately with the salad.

CHOCOLATE-COVERED ESPRESSO BEAN BROWNIES

Sometimes dessert needs a kick: Smashed-up espresso beans and deep dark chocolate will awaken the flavor of these fudge-like brownies (and keep you wide awake as well).

1 cup (2 sticks/225 grams) unsalted butter, cubed, plus more for greasing

6 ounces (170 grams) bittersweet chocolate (60 to 72 percent cacao), coarsely chopped

2 ounces (55 grams) unsweetened chocolate (90 to 100 percent cacao), coarsely chopped

1 ¼ cups (165 grams) all-purpose flour, sifted

1 teaspoon baking powder

½ teaspoon salt

2 cups (370 grams) granulated sugar

4 large eggs

2 tablespoons instant espresso powder

1 teaspoon pure vanilla extract

½ cup (85 grams) chocolate-covered espresso beans, coarsely crushed*

Preheat the oven to 350°F (180°C) and grease a 9-by-13-inch (23-by-33-centimeter) baking pan with butter.

Melt the cubed butter and chocolates in a medium heat-proof bowl set over a saucepan of barely simmering water, stirring occasionally until smooth.

In a small bowl, whisk together the flour, baking powder and salt. In another bowl, whisk together the sugar and espresso powder first, then add the eggs and vanilla and whisk to combine. Add the flour mixture and crushed chocolate-covered espresso beans and whisk to combine. Pour the batter into the prepared baking pan, spreading it in an even layer.

Bake until the sides begin to pull away slightly and a toothpick inserted into the center comes out clean with a few moist crumbs attached, 25 to 30 minutes. Allow the brownies to cool completely in the pan placed on a wire rack, then cut into 24 squares.

* To coarsely crush the chocolate-covered espresso beans, place them in a sealable plastic bag and smash them with a rolling pin.

WORDS
JULIE POINTER

PHOTOGRAPHS
RAHEL WEISS

STYLING
ROSE FORDE

The Language of Limbs

Folded arms, clenched fists and crossed legs can communicate our feelings more loudly than words: Learning to control the way our limbs convey meaning gives us greater control of our messages. What language is your body speaking?

Every day we perform a careful monologue with our bodies, communicating our inner thoughts in smiles, shrugs, slouches and glances. Our conscious minds are often not even aware of these somatic signals, meaning our physical movements can reveal our deepest beliefs: A wide stance and open arms can project certainty within calamity by allowing our innermost convictions to speak through us, while those who communicate with stiff or wooden bodies show a lack of belief in their own words. We may try to speak outwardly with a sense of bravado, but a nervous fidget and downcast eyes can reveal the deep-seated fear within. Conversely, those who are fluent in the subtleties of body language stand out with quiet confidence and possess a mastery of silent communication. Consciously or not, we express a level of emotional intelligence through the use of nonverbal signs. Aside from learning how to listen to our own motions, replicating the gestures of those around us can also teach us empathy. Just as we parrot the vocal inflection and cadence of those we're listening to, we momentarily share another's joy when we mirror a smile, or experience another's sadness through a furrowed brow or unexpected tears. By grasping the power of body language, we not only better convey our own feelings, but also gain the ability to more fully understand the meaning of the postures of those around us. Even people who are naturally predisposed to closing themselves off through crossed arms and hunched shoulders can train their bodies toward the common language of confidence by maintaining eye contact, posturing an open stance and lending gestures of affirmation like nodding or extending an arm. By learning the linguistic nuances that we communicate through movement, we can each find a dialect of our own and begin to speak our way toward tangible courage.

WORDS
GAIL O'HARA

PHOTOGRAPHS
NICOLE FRANZEN

A Toast to Tradition

Family. Quality. Service. Smoked fish. History. Soul. Bagels. New York. Community. Few businesses embody these qualities as perfectly as the 101-year-old "appetizer" shop Russ & Daughters on the Lower East Side. We speak to the fourth generation running the institution.

When Joel Russ emigrated from Austria-Hungary to the United States in 1907, he kicked off his career by selling strings of mushrooms that he carried on his shoulders. After running his business out of a pushcart and then a horse and wagon, Joel was able to open up his first brick-and-mortar "appetizer" shop in 1914 (first on Orchard Street in the Lower East Side, and later at the current location on East Houston Street in 1920). During this time he and his wife, Belle, had three daughters: Hattie, Anne and Ida. Hattie began learning the business in 1924 and her sisters came in to help shortly after. The shop was renamed "Russ & Daughters" in 1933, which caused quite a ruckus in the neighborhood—women just didn't run businesses in those days. Sadly, Joel passed away in 1961, and later Anne's son Mark Russ Federman took over the shop in 1978. More recently, Joel's great-grandchildren Joshua Russ Tupper and Niki Russ Federman (pictured) have been handed the torch to run, expand and modernize the store. R&D has been through a lot: During the Depression, Joel had to decide whether to sell the business or the family home, and he opted to sell the house, betting that saving the business would keep the family afloat. And now, 101 years later, Russ & Daughters is still going strong.

R&D sells *forshpayz*, which means the foods you eat with bagels, such as smoked or cured fish, homemade salads and cream cheese. In 2014, the year that the original store celebrated 100 years in business, Niki and Joshua decided to open a new sit-down café on Orchard Street, very close to their great-grandfather's original space (they also plan to open a shop/café in the Jewish Museum this spring). R&D has a loyal following that includes Maggie Gyllenhaal and Justice Ginsburg, and was also the subject of a documentary called *The Sturgeon Queens* in 2014. We interviewed cousins/fourth-generation owners Niki and Joshua about small-business longevity, family traditions and smoked fish.

What kind of experiences did you have in the shop as a kid? — *Josh*: We'd go behind the candy counter, fill our pockets and then go to my grandmother's house and have a big Russ & Daughters spread for lunch. My cousin and I would take bagels, put cream cheese on them and then proceed to put every single fish on top. My grandmother would yell at us: "How are you going to taste everything with salmon and sable and sturgeon and herring all on the same bagel?!"

Do you know of any other stores with "& Daughters" in the name? — *Niki*: As far as we know, it was the first business in this country with "& Daughters," and it's still rare. You mostly see "& Sons," "& Brothers," "& Cousins." I'd like to think my great-grandfather was this pioneering feminist making a political statement, but the sad truth is that he didn't have any sons: He only had daughters. He also understood that it sounded like a good name, and maybe it wasn't so bad if he stirred up a bit of controversy, which he did.

What are the challenges of running a family business? — *Niki*: R&D is in a very rare minority of fourth-generation businesses. I've heard that only 1 percent of family businesses ever make it to a fourth generation. I joke that the secret to running a successful family business is to not have too much family involved. But there's a benefit because there's a level of trust there, which is hard to come by: Josh and I can cover for each other. In some family businesses there's pressure or expectation on certain family members that this is something you have to do with your life, and that's unfair. At some point people will realize that they're not living the life they wanted. We have a very individualistic society and you're supposed to do your own thing, not what your parents did. I had that prejudice for a long time, but traveling to Asia and Europe where I saw family businesses that have been going for ten generations made me appreciate the beauty of being part of a legacy. A family business can't be a birthright. I didn't inherit anything—I had to work hard and prove I was capable of doing this.

What has the family business taught you about longevity? — *Niki*: The importance of taking the long view. We feel more like stewards who are entrusted with preserving and growing R&D so we'll be able to hand it off to the next generation—of our family and our customers. We're making decisions that will ensure the business will be around for another 100 years. Our longevity is due to quality.

R&D has continuously been a part of New York history and a part of people's lives for so long that it has become a geographic and emotional reference point. It helps people make sense of their lives. The second you step into R&D, you're transported. It conjures up a memory: Where you went as a kid or eating with your grandparents or when you lived in New York. A guy walked in the door not too long ago and we kept saying, "Can we help you?" And he just stood there and said, "Can I just stand here for a second? I'm just so happy that you're still here." It's more than just a store—it feels like a community center.

You guys took over the business but also opened a new one, the Russ & Daughters Café. Do entrepreneurial qualities run in your family? — *Josh*: It comes naturally to me. Even with inheriting a 100-year-old business, you need to grow the business and see the future. We determined that it was time to open a sit-down restaurant. From the family's perspective, it has always just been a store, so there was pushback. You have to be comfortable with risk. Thankfully we both have the spirit. It's sort of like eye color: Some people get it and some don't.

How's the café going? — *Niki*: It is going great. It's a real fulfillment of a dream. As special as R&D is as a store, a piece of the experience was missing because so many people went there wanting to

stay, wanting to bring their friends and family and linger. We knew it had to be a space that would be as welcoming to the babies, the hipsters, the altacockers [the old-timers] and three generations sitting down at the same time. People are coming to the café to celebrate their weddings, anniversaries and family reunions.

What were some of the little things you changed? — *Niki*: We've made a lot of changes to modernize R&D, but the test for whether a change has been successful is if nobody notices. When I came on board a few years after Josh, we were still taking orders with a pen and paper. We now have a fully integrated point-of-sale system and web orders are integrated with store orders. Most customers don't notice because they're still talking to a person on the phone and it's probably the same person who took their order three months ago. There's still this very human element.

Do you have any good stories about regulars? — *Niki*: So many! First of all we joke that if you've been coming for less than 20 years, you're a new customer. One customer who had been introduced to the store by her husband used to come every Friday. She was a regular for 30 years, and José was the only person who would slice for her—they had this over-the-counter love affair going on. Then she started battling cancer: She couldn't come in, but we would deliver to her. When she passed away, her daughter called and said, "My mother wrote a list of people she wanted to be informed that she'd passed away, and Russ & Daughters was one of them." Things like that happen all the time. People bring in their girlfriends and want to introduce them to the guys across the counter to make the relationship official. People come in and they tell me about my grandparents or my great-grandparents.

What is so special about your relationship with the customers? — *Josh*: It goes back to the banter and interaction and relationships we have with the people that have come in every week for 60 to 80 years, or maybe just a few years. We want the customers to feel like they're a part of our family. We're a very important part of people's lives, maybe because we provide food for bar mitzvahs, bat mitzvahs, weddings, shivas, all these stages of life.

What kind of family rituals and traditions do you have? — *Niki*: The irony of growing up in R&D is that people assume I had these outrageous brunches all the time and our holidays must have been over-the-top, but the reality was that my parents were always working, and when we were old enough, we were working too. One tradition we have is on New Year's Eve: We close the store at 6 p.m. and—as a family—we open up a tin of caviar, spoon it out on mother-of-pearl spoons and have some champagne. It just reminds ourselves: "Right, this is so delicious."

RUSS & DAUGHTERS' POTATO LATKES

These comforting potato pancakes have traditionally been served during Hanukkah, though latkes have come to represent celebration in all its forms. Serve these fried morsels with either sweet or savory toppings.

2 ½ pounds (1.2 kilograms) Idaho russet potatoes

1 medium yellow onion

2 large eggs, separated

½ cup (40 grams) finely chopped scallions

¼ cup (35 grams) matzo meal (or potato flour)

3 tablespoons unsalted butter, melted

2 teaspoons kosher salt

½ teaspoon freshly ground pepper

¼ teaspoon baking powder

Vegetable oil, for frying

Optional toppings:
— Applesauce
— Sour cream
— Thinly sliced Scottish smoked salmon
  and crème fraîche
— Wild Alaskan salmon roe and crème fraîche
— Trout roe and crème fraîche

Place a large strainer over a large bowl. Using the large holes of a box grater, grate some potato, followed by some of the yellow onion, into the strainer. Repeat until all of the potatoes and onion have been grated. (Alternating the potatoes and onion prevents the potatoes from discoloring.)

Squeeze or press out as much liquid as possible. Allow the accumulated liquid to stand in the bowl for 2 to 3 minutes. Once settled, pour off the watery part, but reserve the thick starchy paste at the bottom of the bowl.

Transfer the potato-onion mixture to a clean, large bowl. Add the starchy paste, egg yolks, scallions, matzo meal (or potato flour), butter, salt, pepper and baking powder, and mix well.

In a separate medium bowl, beat the egg whites with an electric mixer until they hold stiff, shiny peaks. Fold the egg whites into the potato mixture.

Heat a thin layer of oil in a large frying pan over medium-high heat. Working in batches, scoop ¼ cup (55 grams) of the potato mixture into the pan for each latke. Flatten gently with a spatula. Fry until the latkes are crisp and golden brown, 3 to 4 minutes per side.

Serve immediately with desired topping, or reheat in a 350°F (180°C) oven, for about 5 minutes.

A Creative
Escape

Leaving your usual environment and venturing out into nature can
often lead to bright ideas and a refreshed imagination. We follow
film directors Andrew and Carissa Gallo as they head out into Oregon's
rich landscape to work on a new film project titled Pilgrim.

These images are stills from a short film called *Pilgrim* by Sea Chant, a motion picture and photography studio run by Andrew and Carissa Gallo. Granted a few blank days on their calendars between work projects, they set out into Oregon's diverse landscape to create something wholly their own. Filmed in locations all around the state, the couple and their team drove through the undulating environment, camping and stopping to shoot at whim. "We always try to immerse ourselves in projects that aren't just for clients, but exist purely to grow and learn as artists," Carissa says. "This is one of those."

TO SEE THE FILM IN ITS ENTIRETY, HEAD TO SEACHANT.CO

WORDS
GEORGIA FRANCES KING

PHOTOGRAPHS
TEC PETAJA

A Day in the Life: Helen Rice

After launching a creative agency at age 23 with her now-husband Josh Nissenboim, Helen Rice is living the entrepreneurial dream. Her company Fuzzco is going swimmingly a decade on—and she still has time for pottery, running and plenty of coffee. We tagged along for a day in her neighborhood of Charleston, South Carolina.

When you have the privilege of calling your creative passion your career, the division between where personal time begins and the emails end is often fuzzy. That's not why Helen Rice named her creative agency Fuzzco, but it reflects the way she's lived her life up until now. Originally setting up shop in a dual work/living space in a 150-year-old house that she and her husband renovated themselves, Helen is learning to balance business with leisure. Fuzzco has now moved into a 7,000-square-foot office in Charleston and employs more than a dozen staff members—leaving the couple to enjoy their sprawling, crumbling home as a work-free sanctuary. Business may be booming, but Helen always manages to make time for coffee on the porch with her cats.

What does your normal weekday morning routine look like? — The past year has been about trying to slow down and take more time for myself, so I'm transitioning from an allowance of 30 minutes from eyes open to stepping into the office to a more luxurious hour and a half—sometimes two—to get going in the morning. I love getting up earlier than my husband Josh when the house is quiet, getting a run in and making some coffee. I've been taking pottery classes so I've made a lot of mugs, and I like choosing a different one to drink out of each morning. If there were an action figure version of me, her accessory would be a coffee cup. I'll then sit with my two cats and read the paper—we get the Sunday *New York Times* and I'll read it throughout the week. I purposefully don't look at email until I've had my run and read a little bit of the paper, because once I'm tending to my email, that's it, I'm sucked in. Josh—who I started the business with—and I then walk to the office together. It's about an eight-minute walk, or a four-minute jog if we're cutting it close! We'll often see people we know in the neighborhood and a ton of squirrels.

Please describe your home. — We live downtown in a traditional Charleston-style stand-alone house that was built in 1852. I grew up nearby in another Charleston stand-alone house, so the layout and the well-worn traditional details are nostalgic for me. It's very drafty though—you can see straight through the first floor's floorboards to the dirt below. But there's something humble about the old, unfinished, drafty building that I love. We bought it about five years ago and it has been—and always will be—a work in progress. It's like a wooden boat, as there is constant maintenance and the structure is somewhat delicate. I couldn't imagine ever being done with the house, and I really enjoy the little transformations over time.

What do you enjoy about running? — I'm an introvert, so I need time to quietly process things. Running is meditative for me. I've been doing it since high school and I love it as it really chills me out. I'm easily distracted, but I find I can focus better during the day if I've been on a run. I go in the mornings because I know I'll actually *do it* if I do it first thing, but I prefer to run at night when all of the houses are lit up. I go for three to five miles on average—sometimes I'll go longer, but my body gets mad at me.

How did you become interested in pottery? — I focused on drawing and painting after school but I hadn't been able to get back into it. I wanted to make things with my hands again and I've always loved utilitarian sculpture, so pottery seemed like the perfect outlet. When I'm in class, I don't think about work and I get to make things for our house—mostly vessels like mugs and vases. Everyone makes the Demi Moore/Patrick Swayze joke when I tell them!

You're an avid gardener too: What is it about flowers and vegetables that makes you feel grounded? — It's the same thing as pottery and running: My mind wanders and I don't get hung up on one particular thought. I could spend half the time digging or weeding and half the time looking at the bugs and taking note of new things happening in the yard. Sometimes I'll find dead birds or a pack of kittens. I really like finding kittens.

What is Fuzzco? — It's a creative agency where we build brands and create visual and digital experiences. We help interesting companies do interesting things.

What were you doing before you started Fuzzco? — After I graduated in 2003, I spent the next two years making art and trying to sell it. Josh and I had been dating since 2000 and he was also into making websites at the time, so we decided that it would be fun to work together. That was 2005 and we were 23. We only had one computer for the first while and we'd take shifts to work. It took us two years to build the business to a point where we didn't have to work other jobs, but we never got a business loan. We started hiring people at year four, and we've had our 10-year anniversary in January 2014 with 18 staff! We hired amazing people who are better than us at things.

You have chickens at your office instead of your home: Why did you make this choice? — I've wanted chickens for a long time and we all wanted an office pet, so it made sense to have them at the office where there are more people to enjoy them. We go home for lunch every day and usually take some eggs with us and cook them up with some greens! Getting out of the office is such a breath of fresh air and really helps provide perspective. It also gives us a chance to be with our two old cats and sit on our porch in the sun.

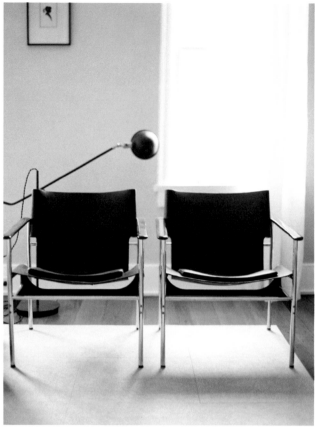

Please tell us more about your office space. — Our office is more than 7,000 square feet: one big rectangle with a parking lot in the front and a long sliver of land behind where we keep the chickens. Upstairs is dedicated to making work and downstairs is a mix of meeting spaces, a kitchen, library, lounge and a room to make things with our hands.

What kinds of challenges came with starting a company with your husband? — Josh and I met in our sophomore year of college in Minnesota in fall 2000 and got married in 2010. He took me out for coffee and cake and we've been hanging out since. I feel very lucky to be able to work with him and it certainly has its advantages. We can work longer hours and process ideas when we aren't actively working. The only disadvantage is that it's hard to get away from work: Perspective is so important, and creating distance from work helps us see the big picture. I think we could have more of that.

How are you trying to achieve a better work-life balance? — We're in a phase right now where the heat is on. Some really exciting things are happening and constant emails are inevitable. There are times when I can get away though: If I make a commitment to be away from technology at a certain time, I'll be more productive to make it happen. I also started leaving my phone at home when I'm not working, as even checking in for four or five minutes here and there can really drain my energy and pull me out of the moment.

What strategies do you implement to foster a healthy working environment? — We're very organized, but we're definitely not serious all the time. There is plenty of teasing, terrible bets, dares, people playing pranks and all kinds of shenanigans. We make sure that every hour is accounted for during our resources meetings: This way people know what they should be doing at any given moment and it also gives us a ton of control over how much we work or don't work. People rarely work late because we've made sure that they won't have to by scheduling enough time to complete their tasks within the normal workday.

Do you usually go out for dinner, or do you cook at home? — We're normally home for dinner. Josh is the cook and I'm the cleaner. He's always making something. Cooking is his chance to clear his mind and I'm happy to eat anything he makes me. We also have people over a lot: We love to play games, so often a night won't end before we've played either Catan, Carcassonne or Yaniv.

What is it about Charleston that speaks to you? — I was born and raised about 10 blocks from where I live now. I love it: the salty air, the humidity, the hot summers, the old houses and their yards that haven't been manicured. Thinking about what the city was like when I was growing up makes me think of quieter times when I didn't have so much to care or worry about. Charleston is small and relatively simple if you let it be, and I like that.

ILLUSTRATIONS
SARAH MAYCOCK

WORDS
ALYX GORMAN
JOANNA HAN
PANICHA IMSOMBOON
TARANEH JERVEN
GEORGIA FRANCES KING

ANNA LOH
SAMMI MASSEY
GAIL O'HARA
SARAH ROWLAND
KATHERINE SACKS
PICO WRIGHT

The Community
Entrepreneurs

When we think about the entrepreneurs that inspire us, the companies and individuals that come to mind not only focus on creating imaginative goods and services but also support and foster their local communities. The following 25 business folks bring people together, and we think they deserve an appreciative round of applause.

THE MAKERS

Whether they create products with a conscience, revive classic communication or give choice back to consumers, makers can also be social doers.

APOLISGLOBAL.COM

APOLIS

These Los Angeles–based brothers empower the global creators and communities behind their clothes.

When brothers Shea and Raan Parton traveled to underdeveloped countries as kids, they didn't realize that seeing the similarities and differences in cultures across the globe would drive them to build a social corporation that provides impoverished people with equal access to the global market. Years later, they based their lifestyle brand and family operation Apolis on a business model that strives for advocacy through industry. "The idea was that the textile and garment industry could create jobs around the world, especially in countries that are stuck in the poverty cycle," Shea says. "It could've been any business, actually—as long as it serves the purpose of improving people's lives." Apolis teams up with a diverse range of employees around the globe to manufacture their products, from vegan bag makers in Bangladesh to shoemakers in the West Bank. Despite the company's success, Shea reiterates the importance of being grounded: "Surround yourself with people who care more about your health and sanity than your creative ideas—that is ultimately what success is about." AL

RIFLEPAPERCO.COM

RIFLE PAPER CO.

Anna Bond is enlivening the time-honored art of letter-writing through her illustrated designs.

"I hope seeing a beautiful card in a shop inspires people to write a note to someone they care about," says Anna Bond (pictured). She opened her nostalgic paper goods company in 2009 with her husband, Nathan, despite fewer people using old-fashioned mail. "Stationery is something that will always have a place, even if it changes meaning, style and how we approach it," she says. Anna had been working as a freelance designer and illustrator when some friends asked her to design their wedding invites. That's when she found her calling: "There wasn't anything like my illustration style in the paper industry at the time," she says. Rifle Paper Co. creates colorful greeting cards, journals, wrapping papers, art prints, phone cases, recipe boxes and other goods that are sold online and at more than 4,000 retailers around the world. "We honestly didn't have a grand plan when we started," she says. "We knew we were starting something special but never dreamed where it would take us. I definitely dream big, but we try to stay receptive about what steps we're taking to get there." GO

WEARGUSTIN.COM

GUSTIN

This menswear brand uses a crowd-controlled business model to create less waste and happier customers.

Gustin is not a typical menswear retailer—it only manufactures products if its customers choose to back them. The company designs mocks that consumers vote on: If a piece gets enough backers, it will be made, meaning consumers get what they want and Gustin doesn't end up with a pile of shirts no one wishes to buy. Cofounder Josh Gustin previously sold through high-end boutiques but found the experience lacking. "Selling jeans for more than $200, guessing what people wanted to wear and being at arm's length from the consumer felt incredibly inefficient," he says. Josh relaunched Gustin in 2011 with Stephen Powell, a new distribution model and radically reduced prices. For their new venture, being responsive to their community is a priority. "If your relationships with your customers are an afterthought, people pick up on that and see that you're not genuine," Stephen says. "The old world of fashion is a bit standoffish—it's about creative geniuses who you can't interact with or understand—you feel lucky to be able to buy their products. We go out of our way to do the opposite." AL

THE STORE OWNERS

Neighborhood shops don't just provide goods and services: They can also become valuable support structures within creative communities.

THISOPENSPACE.CA

THIS OPEN SPACE

Yashar Nijati provides a storefront and economic opportunities to forward-thinking small businesses.

Equal parts pop-up shop, matchmaker and publicist, This Open Space is a rotating shop front in Vancouver, BC, that serves as a rolodex for fresh local ideas. Founder Yashar Nijati (pictured) gives a voice to many small-business owners who can't afford their own brick-and-mortar stores and provides a venue for eclectic short-term art ventures. More than 70 different projects have taken over the space since its 2012 launch to introduce new brands and ideas to the community. "We purposefully don't set limitations because people have wild ideas," Yashar says. "If you foster them and provide the framework for them to flourish, they will." A chef-curated Japanese knife boutique, an owner/dog portrait studio and an elopement-style wedding chapel are among the concepts that have made a home in This Open Space. But perhaps its most famous occupant was Faraday Café, the world's first coffee shop to intentionally repel Wi-Fi and cell-phone signals. Nearly 1,000 people stepped into the void during their two-week installation to enjoy a mug and a face-to-face conversation instead of checking emails. TJ

MAGMABOOKS.COM

MAGMA BOOKS

London-based media figure Marc Valli helps readers reconnect with the printed word as the cofounder of Magma Books and the editor in chief of Elephant magazine.

Opening a bookstore during the height of the digital boom may not have seemed like a smart business decision for some, but for Marc Valli—cofounder of Magma Books and editor in chief of acclaimed art magazine *Elephant*—that was half the thrill. "It's an exciting time, but one in which there are no big established truths," he says. "Everything is up in the air, and therefore up for grabs…" Launching his first store with Montse Ortuno in 2000, Marc now has three Magma Books and one Magma Product shop in the UK. Though many wander inside in search of printed matter, Marc realizes they don't always know which specific title they're seeking, only that they're searching for that feeling of belonging. "Reading a magazine can make you feel more deeply connected with others," the Brazilian-born entrepreneur says. "I remember being younger and not being able to connect with anything around me and then bumping into a magazine and thinking, 'Wow, there are people out there who think, feel and dream like me.' " The open layouts of their stores and the variety of other products they stock—everything from novelty playing cards to contemporary lighting fixtures—encourages visitors to linger and play instead of feeling rushed. Buyers can't find this carefree vibe on the internet, which has helped keep Magma afloat during the tough times. Marc and Montse nearly closed their doors in 2008 after Magma was handed the "perfect storm" of the internet revolution, Amazon's cheaper pricing models and spiraling retail rental rates. But instead of folding, they decided to reinvent the business. "We had no money and it felt like *Mission Impossible*, but we knew it was the only light at the end of the tunnel," he says. If opening his own bookstore seemed like a questionable idea, founding a magazine in midst of a recession and the cries of "print is dead!" was even more outlandish. *Elephant*'s first issue was published in 2009 and became an extension of the non-elitist brand of high art and design that Magma champions. "Nowadays, just about anyone can publish anything online, almost for free and without that much effort," he says. Marc therefore hopes that in a more and more digitalized universe, print will come to stand for quality and commitment: "Time and attention spans are valuable commodities in our day and age, so print still has a few aces in its pack." GFK

THE FOOD ENTHUSIASTS

Food can be used to enrich, strengthen and connect people of all societies and cultures: All you need to share is a passion for tasty morsels and tradition.

BREADFURST.COM

BREAD FURST

At the age of 76, Mark Furstenberg opened a neighborhood bakery in the heart of Washington, D.C.

At the ripe age of 50, Mark Furstenberg decided to switch careers entirely to become a professional baker. "I didn't like what I was doing at the time, writing about other people's experiences," he says of his previous career as a political speechwriter and journalist. "I wasn't finished having experiences of my own." Over the following quarter of a century, Mark became a beacon of great food in Washington, D.C., both as a talented chef with a James Beard Award under his belt and an entrepreneur with a keen sense of creating a community around food. "I don't consider us a walking-shopping city," he says, "but we are making progress as a food city." After founding a local gourmet market chain, a popular restaurant near the White House and a bread consulting agency, Mark honed in on what he most deeply wished to contribute to the D.C. food scene: a neighborhood bakery. At age 76, he followed through with his vision in 2014 by opening Bread Furst. In addition to making top-quality baked goods, Mark spreads the entrepreneurial spirit of the local retailers by taking on apprentices and "making it seem possible for others to open neighborhood stores," he says. "I want to help others achieve what I have." SM

BEERPROJECT.BE

BRUSSELS BEER PROJECT

Olivier de Brauwere and Sébastien Morvan have found a way to make brewing a collaborative effort.

Brewing in Belgium is defined by tradition. The craft dates back to the 1100s when people used to brew beer in church abbeys, and modern Belgian beer tastes are often still characterized by Old World styles today. But brewers Olivier de Brauwere and Sébastien Morvan tossed aside convention when they founded Brussels Beer Project in 2013, combining international inspiration with an innovative crowd-sourced program. "We wanted to involve people as much as possible through crowd-sourcing, crowd-funding, social media and lots of events and opportunities to share our passion face-to-face," Sébastien says. More than 800 of Brussels Beer Project's backers helped choose their first crowd-sourced flavor: a lightly hoppy organic IPA called Delta. The beer lovers not only chose the flavor profile of the brew—a cross between a Hefeweizen and a Tripel—but also named it Grosse Bertha. Thanks to a successful crowd-funding campaign, the team is set to launch its own Brussels microbrewery in 2015, along with a new online platform to further encourage feedback and brewing ideas. "We wanted to involve the community from the start, as we believe it's in the DNA of the project," Sébastien says. KS

MOCHI-KITCHEN.COM

MOCHI KITCHEN

Erino Tezuka Wade's mochi business grew out of her genuine desire for an edible piece of her heritage.

"I usually talk to the mochi and say, 'Please be tasty and make customers happy,'" says Erino Tezuka Wade, a Japanese freelance furniture designer who started Mochi Kitchen in Somerville, Massachusetts, about a year after she moved there from San Francisco. When her first East Coast winter was approaching in 2011, Erino realized it was impossible to find freshly made mochi—Japanese rice paste balls—for a Japanese New Year's soup called *ozoni*. The only option other than buying frozen mochi was making it herself with a small machine she'd received as a wedding gift. Starting as a way to appreciate her heritage, the business has connected Erino with both Boston's Japanese community—which is thrilled to get a taste of home—and curious American customers. Although her rice cakes are mainly made to order, she occasionally offers them at local Japanese events, where she describes the small snacks as "cultural sharing moments" that can introduce the country's traditions to the locals who attend. For Erino, who used to wonder what and how she could contribute to the Japanese community, being the only mochi maker in town gives her a sense of cultural pride as well as a tasty connection to her roots. PI

THE DO-GOODERS

Good business isn't always about financial goals and selling products: These five social enterprises inspire us to give more to our communities and take less.

DETROITSOUP.COM

DETROIT SOUP

Amy Kaherl helps get local businesses off the ground through a combination of public support and hearty soups.

A hot meal and a good conversation are powerful tools for igniting a community. As the leader of Detroit Soup, a micro-grant project that's given more than $80,000 to the revival of the once-bankrupt city, Amy Kaherl knows this concept well. "We felt we could empower and connect the community," she says. Every month, Detroit Soup hosts public dinners in abandoned warehouses where up to 300 locals meet to share ideas. Each person pays $5 to enter and brings a salad or dessert to go with the evening's provided soup: Attendees then present their business concepts, people vote on their favorite idea and the proceeds go directly to the winner, further empowering and fueling the growth of new projects throughout the city. Working with Detroit Soup since its 2011 launch, Amy has watched the organization fund many worthy projects and change lives. "I get to create community conversation and meet some of the most passionate people on the planet," she says. "People are meeting and sharing ideas, jobs are being created and people are doing amazing work in the community." S R

DEPAVE.ORG

DEPAVE

By transforming paved areas into sustainable green spaces, Eric Rosewell enlivens Northwest neighborhoods.

"Ripping up pavement is really fun, and it's a lot easier than you might think," says Eric Rosewell, founder of community refurbishment organization Depave. The company began in 2008 after he and a friend helped tear the pavement out of their yards in Portland, Oregon, in an act of environmental stewardship and camaraderie. Since then, the organization has transformed paved landscapes into beautiful sustainable green spaces all over the Pacific Northwest using the hands of the locals themselves: The community—whether a school, nonprofit or church—assemble volunteers of all ages who help plan and carry out the parking lot's revitalization. "We enjoy giving people a really fun unique experience that clearly makes a difference," he says. In addition to the social benefits of replacing pavement with green space and bringing nature into urban environments, "there's a whole host of environmental benefits that come along with depaving," Eric says, including protecting rivers from pollutant runoff. By working from the grassroots, Depave gets people in touch with their natural neighborhoods. S M

EDIBLESCHOOLYARD.ORG

EDIBLE SCHOOLYARD

As Alice Waters discovered, the best way to educate those in need is to show them how to grow their own produce.

In 1995, chef Alice Waters made a passing comment about an empty lot on King Middle School's campus in Berkeley, California, and decided to transform it into an edible garden that would be integrated into the school's curriculum. Today, that very garden is the Edible Schoolyard's home base where her team develops classes and trains practitioners (and it has developed a school lunch initiative that provides healthy, fresh and mostly organic school lunches for all the Berkeley School District campuses). The Edible Schoolyard Project views gardens and kitchens as dynamic classroom spaces where kids can learn about biology, ecology, history and even math and physics. The lessons children learn by growing, harvesting and cooking healthy meals feed into their communities later on. "The principles of edible education include values of connectivity—nothing is isolated," says Kyle Cornforth, the director of the project. The King Middle School garden is also open to the public during all non-school hours, which "fosters a sense of belonging and ownership for the Berkeley community," he says. S M

> "If you're trying to bring people together,
> it has to be fun. Otherwise people will just
> stay home and watch *House of Cards*.
> I know I would."

JESS MILLER

GARAGESALETRAIL.COM.AU

GARAGE SALE TRAIL

Proving that one person's trash is another person's new wall hanging, Sydney's Jess Miller helped found a nationwide series of garage sales.

Jess Miller and her PR firm Goody Two Shoes have been clicking their heels at the center of some of the most innovative community-focused events in Australia. Growing up on an herb farm, Jess (pictured) learned how to mobilize a crowd as a climate activist. But she's now discovered that the best way to encourage a lot of people to fight tough issues such as climate change is by building what she calls a Trojan Horse of Fun. "Most of the time, people will come to you with a problem like climate change, poverty, disease—really depressing stuff," she says. "So you have to trick them into doing what you want without opening your mouth." By shrouding a serious message in fun, Jess has had great success with many of her projects. She is a founding member of the Garage Sale Trail, an annual event that is hosted on thousands of front porches nationwide: Participating houses are featured on a huge interactive map to encourage locals to interact with their neighbors and reuse each others' wares. "I use the internet to get people off the internet," Jess says. And it works: 350,000 people attended the last Garage Sale Trail. Another one of her Trojan Horses Grow It Local: As a way to encourage neighborhood sustainable food practices, she encourages people to grow vegetables in exchange for tickets to a fancy meal made using those very plants. "I don't create events that I personally wouldn't want to participate in," she says. "If you're trying to bring people together, it has to be fun, otherwise people will just stay home and watch *House of Cards*. I know I would." And how does she do that? "Generally it involves a seemingly ridiculous idea, a whole lot of hustle and always culminates in a party," she says. "Always a party." AG

VIGNETTES.US

VIGNETTES

Curator Sierra Stinson was tired of waiting for Seattle's art world to open up for unknown artists, so she opened a gallery in her living room instead.

Disappointed with the lack of noncommercial art spaces in Seattle, curator Sierra Stinson was sitting in her near-empty studio apartment when she had the idea of turning her private home into a pop-up gallery. "There's something about inviting the public into your home that instantly creates a nurturing space for the viewer and artist," she explains. "It's easy to talk to the artists if they are standing in a tiny kitchen with you pouring wine into a mug." Every few weeks since 2010, she has opened the doors to her home for one night only to hold Vignettes, a micro-gallery show featuring a selection of underrepresented artists. This not only gives contemporary artists a chance to show their work, but also acts as an opportunity for the local art community to have a non-intimidating space to mingle. "I found that having a gallery in your home bridged a gap between the 'art world gallery interaction' and the 'real world interaction'. It humanizes everything and is no longer this talk of the elite," she says. "It's not like walking into a white cube gallery with an attendant behind a computer at a desk." Sierra is also in the process of developing an online version of the project called Vignettes Collection. By reevaluating the current gallery structure in both physical and digital form, more opportunities are arising for artists to both connect with potential buyers and foster a compassionate scene. Even though she is at the center of a creative panorama where competition can be brutal, Sierra believes that authentic face-to-face connections will encourage inter-artist support instead of dissolving it: "I believe the best way to connect is through attendance. Find your community, your people, your place and embrace." GFK

THE CONNECTORS

These two design powerhouses illustrate how bringing together different types of creative communities can foster an innovative and supportive environment.

CREATIVEMORNINGS.COM

CREATIVE MORNINGS

SwissMiss blogger Tina Ross Eisenberg plays Tetris with creatives as the founder of this breakfast-time lecture series.

You may know Tina Ross Eisenberg (pictured) from one of her many creative outlets: She is the voice behind the well-known design blog SwissMiss, the creator of the world's largest temporary tattoo company called Tattly and the force behind StudioMates, a co-working space based in Dumbo, Brooklyn. A connector of creatives, ideas and adhesives, she is the founder of a breakfast lecture series called CreativeMornings, which forms a sense of camaraderie between different creators from all over the world. For one Friday morning a month in more than 100 cities world-wide, hundreds of creatives flow into an event space to hear a series of inspiring themed lectures delivered by some of the industry's most imaginative souls. Tina firmly believes that real connections are made in person and not behind a computer screen, which is why she has expanded the scope of her project to locations such as Lima, Peru, and Bangalore, India. The open nature of the free events mean that CEOs wind up sitting next to students, breaking the conventional barriers between the design hierarchy. "The days of being part of one particular guild are gone," she says. "We shouldn't be living in isolated silos of just information architects or just graphic designers. Magic happens when all of our creative trades connect." She believes that by keeping CreativeMornings free, it instills a level of trust between her and the people who attend, saying that "trust breeds magic." With that in mind, Tina believes we should surround ourselves with people who share our common goals. "The key to life is to find like-minded people who make you feel safe and lift you up," Tina says. "Who you hang out with and surround yourself with will shape you, your dreams and what you collide with." GFK

ADXPORTLAND.COM

ADX

By sharing tools and knowledge, Kelley Roy's Portland, Oregon–based workshop helps form a collaborative community of makers.

Operating out of a 14,000-square-foot warehouse in southeast Portland, ADX is a shared workshop facility and community hub that brings together teachers, experts, makers and youths to make products, develop skills and hang out with other designers. "I really wanted to mash a bunch of disciplines together under one roof," says founder Kelley Roy. "I wanted to involve people with different experience levels to give everyone an opportunity to start working with their hands." ADX offers classes in welding, upholstery, digital design, wooden surfboard making, 3-D printing, laser cutting, design and fabrication, CNC routing, Autodesk and more. Makers can also buy a membership to gain access to the plethora of tools and machines on hand as well as glean advice from others working around them. "A bike builder might be getting feedback from a straight razor maker," Kelley says. "Or a furniture maker might be troubleshooting a certain joint and ask a master craftsman hobbyist, 'What would you do here?' There's a lot of that informal, unstructured learning and sharing of knowledge." While setting up ADX in 2011, she crowd-sourced ideas from the community by inviting students, designers and all the potential target audiences they thought would use the space to come in, see what they liked and tell her what was missing. These days ADX has 13 full-time staffers, many part-timers and more than 200 members all working alongside each other in a very supportive environment. "They're there for their own reasons and their own businesses, but they're also taking care of each other and the space," she says. "People are really thinking outside of themselves, which I enjoy because I think the world needs more of that." GO

THE ONLINE COMMUNITIES

With so many people turning to the internet for a modern sense of community, the challenge becomes connecting those users in real life too.

VSCO.CO

VSCO

Greg Lutze (pictured) and Joel Flory founded VSCO, the art and technology company behind the well-known mobile app and digital photography community.

What does community mean to you? — True community is never manufactured or marketed. It evolves over time and is rooted in honesty and selflessness. It's never "built" by one person, but out of a symbiotic relationship between people who have a binding, driving vision for something greater than themselves. It's inherently greater than the individual. While this is a simple concept, it's something often forgotten as people or brands become focused on themselves and what can be gained.

Describe your relationship with your users. — VSCO is part of the creative class, not above it. We are one and the same. We won't attain success on the backs of the people who we serve and support our mission. If we win, we win together. We stand beside all those that create with reckless abandon—this is our community. We didn't create it, but we hope to help continue to build it.

What are some ways that you cultivate creativity? — We're interested in championing art and artists by equipping, inspiring and promoting creative individuals around the world. With this intent, we highlight innovative photographers, illustrators, designers, painters and artists of all genres on our Journal (vsco.co/journal). We also curate a daily gallery of exceptional images from people around the world on Grid (vsco.co/grid).

How do you allow your users to interact with each other in a unique way? — Our community is largely international—80 percent is outside of the United States—so the opportunity to find and interact with a genuinely global community is high. We curate and feature many of these "undiscovered" talents, highlighting their work to the community and brands. Additionally, the ability to search for people, photos and Journal posts allows for people to discover and connect with others. VSCO helps make photography accessible to anyone, anywhere. Many people would—or could—not purchase a laptop and expensive camera, but they can still create compelling images with the phone they carry in their pockets.

What makes VSCO stand out from other image-sharing platforms? — The exclusion of social clout in the form of likes and comments on VSCO Grid allows for a clear focus on what's important: the creation of original work based on what an individual finds inherently beautiful, real or worth noting. As a result, the images shown on Grid often are honest, artistic moments that would likely not "perform" well on social media platforms. VSCO has never desired to be a "social network." We're not interested in fostering a popularity contest based on likes and comments.

How do you translate your online presence into real life? — Whatever the context, we speak to the same human desire: to know and to be known. Whether we communicate via text or across a table, our desire for connection is unchanged. We're complex humans with emotional insecurities who long to be accepted and desire to be part of something bigger than ourselves. We're interested in the physical manifestation of community where people can interact and establish relationships by engaging in open dialogue. JH

> ## "As Thomas Edison famously said, 'Genius is 1 percent inspiration and 99 percent perspiration.' "
>
> SCOTT BELSKY

BEHANCE

Scott Belsky, the mind behind the portfolio-sharing website Behance and its conference series 99U, explains how he tries to help creatives conquer all obstacles.

What propelled you to create Behance? — The idea was inspired by the frustration felt by my friends in the creative world who complained about the endless obstacles that inhibited their progress. Those people were suffering from inefficiency, disorganization and a lack of attribution for their work. Behance started as a series of experiments to solve this problem. Our team is now concentrated on connecting the creative world and building a leading platform to showcase and discover creative work.

What is the purpose of the design conference series and website 99U? — As Thomas Edison famously said, "Genius is 1 percent inspiration and 99 percent perspiration." To make great ideas a reality, we must act, experiment, fail, adapt and learn on a daily basis. For truly creative people, it's often not the ideas that are the hardest to come by: It's the execution. New ideas are extremely exciting but distracting. Being "idea-driven" is like being drunk—it's a fun but unproductive state. Most companies fail because they attempt to execute too many ideas. So 99U is all about the "perspiration" in making ideas happen: We're trying to help people be better leaders of their own careers.

What are some simple mistakes that entrepreneurs make when trying to grow businesses? — Young creatives often forget that 50 percent of their job is marketing: making sure that their work is showcased well, attributed properly and their audience is growing. Unfortunately, great work doesn't market itself. It's amazing to me how many online portfolios are out-of-date: The common excuse is that "I'm too busy to update my website." But the world is full of noise, and each of us must invest in telling our story and showcasing the work we're capable of. Your potential is limited only by the opportunities you receive from the world around you.

We're often told that if we love what we do and try our hardest, success will come to us, but this is sadly not often true. What message would you prefer to send to young creatives? — It starts with how you define success. To me, success is making an impact in what matters most. If I engage, learn and make an impact by doing something I really care about, I feel successful. If you love what you do, hours of work pass unknowingly and labor becomes indistinguishably woven with engagement. And if you keep at it, you're bound to stumble upon opportunity, even though it may not be what you expected. So if you're getting started in your career, spend time with stuff you really care about. Find jobs that inch you closer to a labor of love.

What advice can you give people who love what they do so much that they never stop working? — When you love what you do, work is personal. When there are no boundaries between your work and life, you are among the luckiest people on earth. So few people have the luxury of not wanting to look at the clock. Of course, the challenge is to still be present wherever we are. When you're with the ones that you love, you need to be able to compartmentalize your other interests. Like all things in life, establishing work-life balance takes practice and self-awareness. GFK

THE RENTERS & LENDERS

Sharing bikes, swapping homes and lending funds to small businesses: These three companies make a living through temporary transactions.

SPINLISTER.COM

SPINLISTER

This Santa Monica–based enterprise has made bicycle sharing more accessible for many happy cyclists.

When peer-to-peer bike rental start-up Spinlister shut down six months after launching in 2011, no one expected it to be revived months later revitalized and rebranded. "I had no idea how to run a company, but I knew that having a unique name like Spinlister was a valuable asset," says Marcelo Loureiro, the driving force behind the revamp. The founders' initial idea was cunningly simple: create an Airbnb-esque service for cyclists to rent users' bikes in different cities and list their own bikes while they travel. But they made a risky decision to suggest the bike-only sharing platform may grow to include other services. Users were baffled by the less-focused new direction, resulting in a temporary shutdown of the company. But Marcelo saw potential, which led him to quietly buy the site and plan an overhaul that would simplify Spinlister's concept. "The community is everything to us," he says. "We learn a lot from it, and it's inspiring that they're rooting for us and helping us out along the way." It hasn't been an easy feat to bring the company back from the app graveyard, but Marcelo is undeterred and believes that Spinlister is on the right track: "Success is when you're happy with what you're doing and have a great perspective of what is ahead of you, even if you're not there yet." AL

COLEANDPARKER.CO

COLE + PARKER

Diana and Jeff House sell socks while simultaneously investing in diverse businesses worldwide.

What do you get when you combine a love for socks, micro-finance and seeding start-ups? The answer is Cole + Parker, a sock business founded by Jeff and Diana House that produces an array of jazzy socks while simultaneously supporting entrepreneurship abroad by handing out small business loans. "When I first traveled to Colombia, I saw the pride that entrepreneurs had who sustained themselves from receiving micro-loans," Jeff says. Named after influential jazz musicians John Coltrane and Charlie Parker—both believers in creativity and the freedom of expression—Cole + Parker runs on a sustainable one-for-many business model, a variation of the one-for-one model made famous by the pioneering socially responsible brand Toms. When a pair of socks is purchased from their website, the funds from that transaction are transferred to Kiva, a micro-finance loan distributor. Kiva then loans out money to an entrepreneur who has applied for business funding in locations from Guatemala to Ukraine. Once the loans are paid back, those funds are then regenerated into helping out yet another entrepreneur. "Currently we've contributed to more than 275 loans," Jeff says. "Each person who has received a loan has had the opportunity to turn his or her life into something better and sustaining." AL

BEHOMM.COM

BEHOMM

Eva Calduch and Agust Juste make affordable house swapping possible for traveling creative professionals.

Behomm is a home-sharing network that believes in more than just free accommodation: "It's about sharing and making personal connections that cross oceans, continents and cultures, making the world a more friendly place," say founders Eva Calduch and Agust Juste. Visual artists and designers can list their homes and organize a house swap with other users worldwide—and neither party needs to pay for it. As seasoned graphic designers and avid travelers, the Barcelona couple formed Behomm to address their own need for such a resource, something that would be like "couch surfing for creatives." They knew that other people would appreciate the opportunity to meet like-minded individuals while receiving—or providing—a beautiful place to stay. "We thought we could link beauty lovers worldwide: designers, visual artists and people with a similar passion for tasteful things and a love for aesthetics," Eva says. "We believe aesthetics have nothing to do with luxury! A tiny home with secondhand furniture can be more tasteful than any castle." Behomm envisions a future of travel that favors sharing friends and homes in an environment of mutuality rather than financial transactions. "Home exchange is about trust and generosity while renting is about earning money," she says. "We want to remain authentic." SM

THE EDITORS

By dreaming up new ways to coach the creative community, these humble scholars are teaching fresh ideas to eager students of all ages.

WILDCRAFTSTUDIOSCHOOL.COM

WILDCRAFT STUDIO

Chelsea Heffner runs a rural creative classroom that aims to combine traditional arts with a little nature.

In 2013, multidisciplinary artist Chelsea Heffner decided to open up her studio in White Salmon, Washington, using the forests and fields as classrooms to teach a variety of programs that creatively dissolve the barrier between nature and our daily lives. "The common thread that links all of our offerings is that each skill requires a certain slowing down and often forces students to reflect on basic elements such as time, weather and geography," she says. Chelsea and her crew of teachers, most of whom work locally as artists, teach a large variety of classes during the warmer months—including those on Natural Dyes, Seasonal Medicine, Mushroom Hunting and Primitive Pottery—and each workshop also includes a home-cooked communal lunch. But for those who don't have the time or geographical means to make it to a session at Wildcraft, Chelsea offers some words of advice for bringing a dose of the wilderness into our daily routines: "Do more! The less time you spend consuming, the more time there is for creating. It almost doesn't matter what it is: Just start making something. Ignore the outcome and celebrate the process." GFK

THEUNIQUECAMP.COM

CAMP

Sonja Rasula's Camp offers eager professionals the tools to make, improve on and sell their wares.

"It's easy to gather people—you just have to decide to do it," says Sonja Rasula (pictured), founder of Camp, a business conference in the woods where creative professionals learn, reflect and network. For four days, campers leave behind their cell phones and computers to reconnect with nature and learn about better business practices in an environment of collaboration and play. "It was really important that I created platforms for entrepreneurs where they could connect, grow and learn through being part of a larger network," Sonja explains. The attendees engage in nostalgic activities such as archery, rope swings and making s'mores while attending workshops on everything from financial practices to social media strategies. "If you create a place for people to meet, gather and mingle, it's shocking how fast community naturally grows," she says. "It's almost instant!" The supportive structure of Camp also lives on in another of Sonja's projects, Unique USA, which is a permanent space in LA's Arts District that encourages both collaboration among makers as well as an interaction between consumers and made-in-America producers. SM

KATEBINGAMANBURT.COM

KATE BINGAMAN-BURT

This trailblazing artist and teacher has a hand in all things graphic design related in Portland, Oregon.

Kate Bingaman-Burt is a design powerhouse in a town full of creatives—a pied piper with a posse of design students trailing her wherever she goes. "Working on a project that's bigger than yourself is a huge community builder, whether it's a portfolio show, lecture series or a publication," says Kate Bingaman-Burt, an associate professor of graphic design at Portland State University. She hadn't planned on becoming an educator, but has a tendency to say "yes" to opportunities that arise. An accomplished illustrator, she is also one of the founders of Design Week Portland and a TED talker. "Some of my happiest moments have been in the classroom making it happen with students," she says. "My mom always tells me I'm a natural-born ham, so that probably helps when teaching." Along with leading classes on branding, strategy, image making and storytelling, she manages an in-house design studio that helps plan events, campaigns and catalogs that the school might require. "It's made me question and grow within my own creative practice simply because it's my job to stay aware so I can help, share and learn along with my students," she says. GO

"We're interested in life's big questions: How we can improve our relationships, find fulfilling work, understand our place in the world and, if necessary, change it."

MORGWN RIMEL

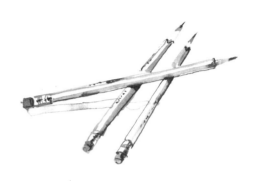

THESCHOOLOFLIFE.COM

THE SCHOOL OF LIFE

The world is full of pseudoscience, bad advice and new age self-help jargon. Thankfully London's School of Life has refreshed the idea of emotional education.

"I'm reminded daily what an ignorant, vain, irritable, choleric idiot I am," says author Alain de Botton when asked what he's learned about himself since founding a school designed to strengthen emotional intelligence. "This is a hugely helpful starting point for the School of Life, for I constantly have ideas about what I—and many other people—might need."

Developed in 2008 by Alain and a group of academics, artists, curators, writers, thinkers and entrepreneurs, TSOL helps people develop emotional intelligence by using culture as a guide. "I came up with the ideas, and the team around me helped to make them happen," he says. "They're brilliant—I owe them so much. Without them, I'd still be a pathetic guy dreaming big." The School offers seminars on such topics as "How Necessary Is a Relationship," "How to Face Death" and "How to Make Up Your Mind," events with speakers such as artist David Shrigley and designer Hussein Chalayan, and you can also drop in for an hour of "therapy" or buy life-improving products in their brick-and-mortar shop.

"Everything we do is driven by a desire to help people derive greater insight into who they are and how they fit into the world," adds Morgwn Rimel (pictured), the School's director. "We're trying to provide a space to think clearly and creatively about the things that matter most. We draw huge inspiration from communities of the past—the universal questions and concerns that humans have grappled with throughout history. We're interested in life's big questions: How we can improve our relationships, find fulfilling work, cope with our anxieties, understand our place in the world and, if necessary, change it." With a team of 15 and a network of faculty, therapists, coaches and partner schools, the London branch

has published 27 books and organized more than 450 events in the past few years. "We're building on the insights and ideas of the great thinkers of the past that still endure and are hugely relevant today," Morgwn says. One recurring event the School puts on is called "Sunday Sermons," which do what churches do: offer instructions in how to live and offer friendship. "However, the content of the sermons is secular—about being kind, about making the most of things, about enduring and about being creative," Alain says. The brand has expanded beyond its London flagship and gone global, with new locations opening in Amsterdam, Antwerp, Belgrade, Istanbul, Melbourne, Paris and Sao Paolo, with others to follow.

The School offers hope to those who struggle in personal and professional relationships, including "culture therapies" such as bibliotherapy and visual arts therapy, mental tune-ups and various downloadable guides to help you navigate a breakup or offer guidance on finding a new job. Students are presented with ideas culled from the humanities (philosophy, literature, psychology, visual arts) in the hope they will help to exercise, stimulate and expand their minds. The team also recently launched School-branded "Tools for Thinking," which are available in other stores, a new YouTube channel with short videos being posted weekly and will soon launch *The Book of Life*, an online editorial platform.

But can emotional intelligence be developed? And even if we attend the correct classes and know what steps to take toward our own happiness, how do we motivate ourselves to change? "Reflect on the brevity of time," Alain says. "We really owe it to ourselves to give it a go." GO

ALAIN
DE BOTTON

Alain de Botton is a one-man media empire, best-selling author and a thinker who uses every possible avenue to apply lessons from history, art, literature and philosophy to everyday problems.

The Zurich-born Alain de Botton was first published at age 23, but it was *How Proust Can Change Your Life*—which applied ideas from the great philosophers to modern-day dilemmas—that made him a best-selling author in 30 countries. The London-based author has written a dozen books on such topics as falling in love, status anxiety and "religion for atheists," become the wise young sage of Twitter and is involved with organizations such as Living Architecture and the School of Life. The latter helps people develop emotional intelligence and become better humans using culture, literature and art as a guide (see previous page). While writing *The Pleasures and Sorrows of Work*, he spent two years talking to people about their workspaces and examining the meaning of work. We asked him about being an entrepreneur and finding meaning in work in modern society.

Do you consider yourself an entrepreneur? — Yes, I am an entrepreneur of sorts—because I took an idea and turned it into a product. It's been a wonderful adventure, and very, very frightening.

Can anybody become an entrepreneur if they have a decent idea? — People tend to say that good ideas are easy to have. I disagree. A really good idea is a very rare thing. I'd reverse the dictum and say that execution is the easy bit—anyone can do it—but unless what you're executing is properly founded, you will fail.

What would the great philosophers say to struggling entrepreneurs? — Philosophy is very concerned with happiness and fulfillment. Therefore, what the philosophers would say above all is: "Are you working on something that can genuinely improve mankind? Are you making a contribution?"

What were some uniting lessons you learned from the interviews you did for *The Pleasures and Sorrows of Work*? — I learned how desperately humans crave "meaning" in their work. What does meaning come from? It comes when you feel that you're somehow improving the lives of others through your work, either by reducing suffering or increasing pleasure. It might be that you're baking cakes or you're helping someone get better from an illness. Humans have a longing to "serve" others. Serving has negative connotations of course, but it is the greatest joy to feel that you have helped other people's lives to go a little better through your talents somehow.

> "It isn't only heroic and glamorous work that counts. The smaller, everyday sorts of work carry just as many chances to do something valuable and good."

ALAIN DE BOTTON

You have mixed feelings about entrepreneurs in the book. What did you discover makes a good entrepreneur or a bad one? — A good entrepreneur has understood human nature and found some bit of our desires or needs to satisfy. A bad entrepreneur has not stopped to ask: "How would my product or service really fit into another person's life?" So the whole thing is extremely psychological below the surface. It's a question of trying to understand the needs of others and to monetize their solutions. Profit might be defined as a way of working out an aspect of other people's needs ahead of your peers.

What characteristics and traits does an entrepreneur need to have? — A powerful imagination and the power to analyze the needs of others and to respond to them through designing products and services around them.

What does a person's workspace say about him or her? — It's no doubt true that the push for open plan office spaces has been led not by an honest assessment of the needs of the worker but because of the desire to save money. It's been dressed up in guff about sharing and being more creative, but everyone knows what's going on. The best sorts of workplaces balance privacy with access: They have a view, solid doors, big tables and good lighting. It costs a lot of money.

Why do we often ask *"what do you do?"* when we should ask *"who are you?"* — The question comes from a financial prejudice, built up because of our reliance on a capitalist model of private enterprise. In this society, an individual doesn't really exist outside of their occupation. You are what you do and what you earn. This is what makes unemployment so tragic—not only are you shorn of money but you are also shorn of an identity and a role in a society that places such store on work.

Is it better to do one job well or to be a multitasker? — Most jobs are really multitasking jobs. You can say that a doctor is just a doctor, but in truth that job involves a hundred different tasks—from being a children's entertainer to a graphic artist to an accountant and so on… So even if we don't want to be, life will push us all to be generalists.

Is perfectionism a positive attribute or a negative one? — It's a positive one, so long as it has borders—that is, so long as we grasp that the whole world, and especially our children and relationships, will never be perfect. But our work does have a chance of having moments of perfection, which is what can make it so compelling.

Does a person's work ethic come from the environment he grew up in or can it be developed? — The origin of the work ethic is fear—fear of being eaten by a bear, by your father's disapproval, by the shame of your society… If you want to get someone to work hard, make sure their parents only loved them in return for performance: They'll be working all hours to prove they have the right to exist and be loved.

How can we learn to leave work at work? — There's no way. Work-life balance is a myth. Anything worth fighting for unbalances you—parenting isn't a hobby, it's a job. You have to make choices, and therefore sacrifices. Having it all exists only in the mind of [Facebook COO] Sheryl Sandberg.

Why is workplace morale important and how can we improve it? — Morale is intangible. It's really about confidence to face challenges. And so often it isn't technical skills we're short of—it's hope. Therefore, a manager who can imbue a team with hope is doing something subtly extremely important: They aren't teaching them a hard skill, yet they are giving them reasons to keep on keeping on.

> **"What does meaning come from? It comes when you feel that you're somehow improving the lives of others through your work, either by reducing suffering or increasing pleasure."**
>
> ALAIN DE BOTTON

How can people maximize the pleasure in their work? — To realize that any task, however mundane, carries with it opportunities for the good things in life: perfection, kindness, precision and beauty. It isn't only heroic and glamorous work that counts. The smaller, everyday sorts of work carry just as many chances to do something valuable and good. I reject this big job/small job dichotomy. It's all one, on a spectrum.

What kind of satisfaction can we get from working? — We're all born with a sense of guilt if we do nothing. It feels dangerous, like we're not properly earning our right to be. Work allows us to exhaust ourselves productively, to bring good to others and thereby feel that we deserve to exist in the community. Also, work keeps us out of trouble—it means we can direct our energies on things that genuinely need doing.

How does unlimited choice affect the career decisions we make? — It panics us. We think, I could be president or Bill Gates or Warren Buffett… Who to be? America imbues people with extraordinary optimism, most of which doesn't bear fruit. It can be cruel, because people are left feeling like they've failed, whereas it is in fact the system that is rigged against them succeeding.

What makes us stay in jobs that aren't right for us? — Fear and a sense we don't deserve better. All of us build up enormous reserves of masochism to keep going, along the lines of: "If it hurts me, it must be good." This can get out of hand.

Have you worked in an office before? What was it like? — All offices are different. The ones I've known have tended to be frenetic places run by tyrants. I learned the value of freedom…

What do you recall of your experience with workplace politics? — The worst thing about work politics is that they're like relationship politics, but you can't just have sex and make up. So things are hard to resolve.

What are some of the pitfalls we fall into when thinking about our careers, and how can we avoid them? — We generally don't think about death enough. We think we're immortal and therefore shirk the really big question which is: "What do I want to do given that life is only 500,000 hours long?"

How do you see your public persona versus your private one? Is it beneficial to make a "character" to show the public? — I think one's public character should be utterly elusive and mysterious. If I was starting again, I'd give myself a bland anonymous name—perhaps Matt Shed—release no pictures, have no backstory, give no readings, never do interviews, and let the work stand for itself. I had no idea how the media worked when I set out at the age of 22.

Where do you write? — I often write in bed, late at night, where it's less scary.

As someone who writes at home, do you have to make an effort to be more social when you're not working? — I've met way too many people in my life. I've traveled the world. Now I'd like more and more to see no one and live as a hermit. It's impossible, but it's my goal. If I live long enough, in my old age, I will go for days without speaking to anyone.

How have you furnished the area around your desk to make yourself feel inspired? — I like to see very little. For me, an inspiring space is one that's totally neutral, because it then allows inspiration in me to come forward. There's nothing worse for good writing than an objectively "pretty scene."

How much of your life is dedicated to writing and how much is spent doing other things? — I run a business called the School of Life. It has grown and grown and it now exists in eight countries and we employ almost 100 people. That's a lot for a writer to take on—and it swallows up a huge amount of time every day.

What other passions do you pursue for either work or pleasure? — My only passion is understanding. I love reading books and acquiring concepts. I'm also very devoted to my family. GO

FOR MORE INFORMATION, VISIT ALAINDEBOTTON.COM

WORDS
JOANNA HAN & ØYVIND HALSØY

PHOTOGRAPHS
KRISTOFER JOHNSSON

STYLING
PER OLAV SØLVBERG

Neighborhood: Sentrum

Nestled between the mountains and the sea in Norway's southwestern archipelago, Bergen is a tiny town known for artistic collaboration. The city center—known to the locals as Sentrum—is home to some of Scandinavia's most community-oriented creative societies, from indie music to innovative local food. We headed there to talk to the locals about the allure of this picturesque town.

"If you drive your car to wherever you go, you don't engage with your neighborhood," says Eirik Glambek Bøe, one half of the indie folk-pop duo Kings of Convenience. "But if you walk and ride your bike, you see people's faces. And the second time you see them, you say hi." A lifelong Bergener with a background in architectural psychology, the singer-songwriter knows a thing or two about how profoundly our environment can influence the way we live and interact with those around us. And in a city as small as Bergen, Norway, this well-balanced sense of physical and social community couldn't be more apparent.

Known simply as Sentrum or "the center," Bergen's tiny central area has geographical boundaries that are defined by striking scenery. The North Sea, the Seven Mountains and dozens of islands stretch out on all sides with everything caught in the middle forming the heart of the city. Sentrum is actually comprised of many smaller neighborhoods—such as industrial Møhlenpris, picturesque Nordnes and lively up-and-coming Skostredet—but in a borough so small that it can be crossed on foot in just 15 minutes, there's a unifying sense of community that's indifferent to formal neighborhood boundaries. Stretching just over ten square miles, these mini municipalities make up 18 percent of Bergen and contain 40,600 of the city's 270,000 inhabitants. With its crooked cobblestone streets, traditional wooden

houses and striking lack of tall buildings, Sentrum can give the initial impression of a charming and sleepy coastal village—but it's precisely the smallness that encourages its inhabitants to turn to each other for collaboration.

Strangers in this city simply can't stay strangers for long. All the photographers, florists, chefs and shopkeepers are bound to be connected in some way, and there's quite a bit of crossover between the many creative communities. A number of stores pair up with other brands for economic reasons, sharing spaces and encouraging interaction between their different patrons. For example, the contemporary art museum Bergen Kunsthall is home to Ink, a bookshop specializing in poetry, art theory and fiction. It also shares a building with Landmark, a popular café, nightclub and event space that hosts everything from drawing clubs to record release parties. Colonialen is another well-loved café with a few different locations around the city, but its space inside the literary arts center Litteraturhuset is a local favorite: Guests can enjoy a plate of smoked salmon on toast and then get lost in the adjoining bookshop or wander upstairs to listen to a writer's seminar.

Other shops combine multiple creative pursuits into one business or simply find ways to extend their presence outside of their immediate fields: Jan Richter Lorentzen, founder of the excellent multiroaster

1   These colorful wooden houses retain the ancient urban structures from the Lower Middle Ages along Bryggen, the old wharf of Bergen.
2   Kaffemisjonen is a quaint café along Øvre Korskirkeallmenning Street that offers barista courses and coffee tastings.
3   Contemporary art museum Bergen Kunsthall functions as a collaborative space, housing a bookshop, café, nightclub and event space.

2

3

1

coffee shops Kaffemisjonen and Blom, is one such proactive contributor to the neighborhood. He spearheads the city's tiny specialty coffee scene by setting up pop-up coffee bars at music festivals, hosting public cuppings and servicing espresso machines for cafés around town.

This collaborative nature is also particularly evident in Sentrum's various fashion businesses. "The atmosphere here is friendly and uncompetitive, so it feels very natural to join forces," says Vegard Moberg Nilsen, owner of the modern clothing retailer Pepper. Featuring a well-edited selection of international designers, Pepper is largely credited with sparking the city's interest in street fashion. He frequently partners with those around him in small but meaningful ways, whether by hiring

local graphic design students to create content for his shop or helping promote new musical talent by inviting bands to perform at store events. Lot 333 is a similar contemporary clothing shop with a focus on European brands, and its neighbors at T-Michael offer expert bespoke tailoring services as well as run the rainwear company Norwegian Rain. High-tech and functional without compromising style, these raincoats are seen all over the neighborhood, sheltering its inhabitants from the 212 days of rain they see each year.

And then there's the city's diverse and internationally renowned music scene. "In a big city, you meet people who share your interests," Eirik says. "In a smaller place, you meet all kinds of people with different interests." Whether they're more inclined

toward dreamy indie-pop, progressive electronica or infamous Norwegian metal, the musicians in Bergen share everything from rehearsal spaces to band members. "We suddenly realized we needed drums in the studio last week," he says. "Within an hour we found a professional drummer who played some beats for us while he was on lunch break from his orchestra." Many people work in close proximity to each other in spaces such as Bergen Kjøtt, a four-story factory building that houses both an event space and studios for more than 300 artists and musicians. Behind the doors of its industrial facade, creativity and collaboration abound: "When so many people are gathered under one roof, grand ideas turn into grand opportunities," says founder Annine Birkeland. "It's common for people

1

1   Nordic restaurant, craft cocktail bar and
    nightclub Lysverket is known for its creative
    fjord-to-table cuisine.
2   The interior of Pepper, a modern clothing
    retailer that carries a well-crafted selection
    from international designers.
3   A customer enjoying coffee in Colonialen
    café and brasserie located inside the literary
    arts center Litteraturhuset.

2

3

to work together here, partly because of the walls—they're not quite soundproof, so things do leak out. The musician John Olav Nilsen often says that hearing others play can either spark a creative partnership or make it clear to you what kind of music you definitely don't want to make!"

Regardless of taste, most Bergeners participate in the music scene in some way, especially students. "A lot of people move here at a young age to study, start a band and then continue to stay," says Henrik Svanevik, owner of the indie book and record shop Robotbutikken. "This makes for a lot of bands, and a lot of bartenders." Making up an entire tenth of Sentrum's population, students are significant contributors to the youthful energy and enthusiasm felt around town. The faculty buildings of the University of Bergen are spread

out all over the city center, so Sentrum itself functions as the university campus.

There's a general acceptance among local small-business owners that in order to grow in such a small borough, everyone must share knowledge, including in Sentrum's culinary sphere. "Luckily, that's also the fun way of working," says Christopher Haatuft, head chef and co-owner of a restaurant called Lysverket. Founded by a mixologist, a musician and two acclaimed chefs, this modern Nordic restaurant, craft cocktail bar and nightclub is just the kind of joint project that thrives here. It's known for excellent drinks and inventive fjord-to-table fare, much of which is prepared with freshly foraged ingredients.

Christopher explains that every chef at every restaurant in town has worked together at some point, so they are all

friends. Rivalry simply doesn't exist. If he's in need of business advice regarding financial matters, he can call up his closest competitor knowing they'll open up. If he comes across an exceptional new supplier of produce, he'll be the first to share the discovery with other restaurants. "The end goal is to encourage innovation and resourcefulness—something that will benefit not just the restaurant, but also the farmer, the farmer's neighbor and our friends at the restaurant next door," he says. "As a city, Bergen is lucky to know that everyone wants everyone else to succeed."

Because large-scale farming isn't easy in a country as hilly and mountainous as Norway, many types of produce are hard to come by. Rather than viewing the agricultural limitations of their landscape as a hindrance to their work, Lysverket

1

2

4

5

1   Inside the Fløibanen funicular that runs
     from the heart of Bergen to the summit
     of Mount Fløyen.
2   A breathtaking view of Bergen from the
     summit of Mount Fløyen.
3   A chef prepares a meal in the kitchen
     of Colonialen café and brasserie inside
     Litteraturhuset.
4   A meal prepared with freshly foraged
     seasonal ingredients at Lysverket, a
     Nordic restaurant, bar and nightclub.
5   Kaffemisjonen's cozy space serves as an
     idyllic spot to sit and sip on coffee while
     people-watching.

3

considers it a chance to embrace the commodities unique to their region and present them in a fresh, elevated light. In Christopher's words, "Why serve foie gras or Bresse chicken when there's mackerel and reindeer right outside our door?"

But Bergeners don't completely romanticize the idea of a small town with a friendly community being able to be totally self-sufficient. The very thing that allows them to be so close-knit and neighborly is also precisely what drives them to look across the North Sea for a breath of fresh air: Their tiny archipelago may restrict urban sprawl within Norway, but their ports also welcome all kinds of international influences right into their hearts.

Bergen has a long history of turning to the rest of Europe rather than inward to their own country for inspiration. With its seagulls, sailboats and colorful wooden houses, Bryggen has served as an important international trading wharf for many centuries. The influence of this period is still evident in the mentality of many Bergeners: They're likely to think and work on a transnational and global scale, and the city has always felt continental and independent of Oslo. "Globalization has made the world a level playing field for creatives," says Eric Amaral Rohter, associate creative director of the communications agency A New Type of Interference (ANTI). Working with clients from all over the world, the company has received many first-place awards for its design, advertising and public relations projects. "Just because we're small doesn't mean we think small. Even though we're here, we think of ourselves as an international agency,"

he says. "Geography is no longer a limiting factor for growth in the creative world, but it does still have a strong influence on creativity and inspiration. By being surrounded by mountains and water, we've developed a creative resilience."

Whether it's the alluring spell of the water and mountains or the unrelenting rain that keeps everyone together inside their studios, shops and kitchens for two-thirds of the year, there is something distinct and energizing in the salty coastal air of Bergen's city center. "We live in a beautiful city that balances nature and human presence, and perhaps that speaks to our work ethic," Eric says. "A great advantage of being here is that a lot of the clutter is taken away. It's easier to see things and have a vision, and there's space to breathe."

Kinfolk Gatherings

As Wendell Berry once said, "A gathering, at its most ordinary, involves hospitality, giving, receiving and gratitude." We would like to thank our community for our past events and look forward to collaborating on many more in 2015.

PHOTOGRAPHS
(Left) Mashiko, Japan: Ryo Shirai
(Right) Lisbon, Portugal: Rodrigo Cardoso—
De Alma e Coração

Over the past four years, *Kinfolk* gatherings have been held in a diverse array of locations and have had all kinds of itineraries. There have been intimate beachside and backyard picnics, boisterous farm feasts and even a skill-based series where we explored topics such as honey harvesting, butchering and the essentials of baking. As the structure of our gatherings continues to grow and change, we strive to keep our most basic goals at the forefront. Our intentions are to inspire our community to continue to slow down, spend more time with friends, family and neighbors, and actively participate in the simple but profound act of gathering around a table.

We're so grateful to all of our hosts, partners, collaborators and attendees who embody the values we hold so dear.

Kinfolk gatherings will continue through 2015 across the globe. For information on upcoming locations, tickets and other details, please keep your eye on our events page.

www.kinfolk.com/events

Event-related inquiries, comments, and simple "hellos" are warmly welcomed at: community@kinfolk.com

ISSUE FIFTEEN CREDITS

SPECIAL THANKS
Thanks to Katrin Coetzer for the Starters and Entrepreneurs illustrations

ON THE COVER
Photograph Pelle Crepin
Styling Aradia Crockett
Photographer's Assistants Filipe Serralheiro and Ian Bird
Hair Yumi Nakada-Dingle
Makeup Joanna Banach at Untitled
Models Charmie and Harvey James
Special thanks to the Russian Club Studios

Clothing
On her: Top by Cos; trousers by Margaret Howell
On him: Jacket by Other Man; shirt by A.P.C.; Trousers by Club Monaco

THE SCIENCE OF SCRIBBLING
Model Josefine Marie Carstad

DEFINING THE ENTREPRENEUR
LEARNING TO UNLEARN
THE PAPER CLIP
CREATIVE CONSTRAINTS
Illustrations Katrin Coetzer

MY BEDSIDE TABLE: THE CURATOR
Special thanks to the Serpentine Galleries, London

FUSION BUSINESSES
Styling Katie Fotis
Special thanks to Gail & Georgia's Facebook friends

THE SOLACE OF SUNDAY NIGHT
Styling Katie Fotis
Pilot Coat Hanger (in teak) Skagerak, designed by Nina Tolstrup

THE LUNCH BOX:
SIMPLE TORTILLA ESPAÑOLA
Lunch box Riess Enameled Two-Tier Tiffin, thanks to Potager NYC
Special thanks to Kacy Strand at Edge Reps

WORK ON YOUR SHOULDERS
Model Caitlin Elisabeth Boucher

IN PRAISE OF SLOWNESS
From the book In Praise of Slowness: How A Worldwide Movement Is Challenging the Cult of Speed *by Carl Honoré. Copyright © 2004 by Carl Honoré. Reprinted by permission of HarperOne, an imprint of HarperCollins Publishers.*

Copyright © 2004 by Carl Honoré. The right of Carl Honoré to be identified as the author of this work as been asserted by him in accordance with the Copyright, Designs and Patents Act 1988.

Production Lottie at Darling Creative
Photographer's Assistant Adam Lang
Digital Operator Oli Geir
Hair and Makeup Lyz Marsden
Model Harry Uzoka at Premier Model Management

Clothing
Page 38, 40, 41, 44, 48: Raincoat by Mackintosh; jacket by Albam; shirt by Margaret Howell; trousers by Folk; shoes and bag by Oliver Spencer

Page 52, 53: T-shirt by MHL Margaret Howell; shorts by Toast

THE PATH TO SUCCESS
Assistant Styling Aartthie Mahakuperan
Photographer's Assistants Bruno Baptista and Tommy Cattanach
Hair Adam Szabó
Makeup Joanna Banach at Untitled
Model Rebeca Marcos at Models 1

Clothing
Page 59: Sweater by Studio Nicholson; trousers by Avelon; shoes by Margaret Howell (worn throughout)

Page 60: Sweater by Paul & Joe; trousers by & Other Stories

Page 61: Top by Studio Nicholson; trousers by Toast

Page 62: Sweater by Loewe; trousers by & Other Stories; waistcoat by Club Monaco

Page 63: Dress by Studio Nicholson; socks by Falke

Page 64: Sweater by ME+EM; trousers by Tibi

COFFEE À LA CARTE
Food styling Camille Becerra
Special thanks to Rob Magnotta at Edge Reps

THE LANGUAGE OF LIMBS
Assistant Styling Indigo Goss
Model Rochana at Premier
Makeup Joanna Banach at Untitled Artists
Hair Maki Tanaka

Clothing
Page 85: Sweater by Joseph; trousers by Toast

Page 86: Top by Gant Rugger; trousers by Folk

Page 87: Turtleneck by John Smedley; top by Rejina Pyo

Page 88: Bodysuit by Wolford; trousers by A.P.C. & Vanessa Seward; belt by Ally Capellino

Page 89: Turtleneck by John Smedley; trousers by Arts & Science; coat by DAY Birger et Mikkelsen

Page 90: Jumpsuit by Album di Famiglia from Egg; coat by Fabio Quaranta

Page 91: Trousers by Toast; shoes by Grenson

A TOAST TO TRADITION
Special thanks to Jen Snow and Julie Cohen

RECIPE: RUSS & DAUGHTERS' POTATO LATKES
Special thanks to Russ & Daughters

THE COMMUNITY ENTREPRENEURS
Special thanks to Linda Derschang, Will Shortz, Nils Bernstein, SHED, Stephanie Rosenbaum Klassen, Fifty Three, The Detroit Bus Company, Islington Community Theatre, Wolverine Farm Publishing, Evan P. Schneider, Grosch, Hiut Denim, Louisa Thomsen Brits

NEIGHBORHOOD: SENTRUM, BERGEN, NORWAY
Special thanks to Ingrid Rundberg, Mikal Tellé, Trude Vaaga, Rikke Helgesen, Frode Boris Bakken and Maren Mosaker

KINFOLK GATHERINGS
Styling Margarida Matias, Mafalda Maya, Mónica Franco, Rita Oliveira – De Alma e Coração and Simply Sebastião
Special thanks to our partners: De Alma e Coração, Simply Sebastião, Casa no Tempo and Anna Westerlund
Painting Satsuki Shibuya and Akio Nukaga
Flowers Chieko Ueno